Mrs Marshall is a Spy

and Other Tales of a Mitchell Boyhood

MERV WELCH

Published in 2022 by L Bell

ISBN:978-0-6454182-0-0

DEDICATION

In memory of my mother, who would have vouched the truth of every word - just because I wrote it.

CONTENTS

INTRODUCTION

This collection of memories has come about in response to the occasional urgings of family and the encouragement of my friends in the Gympie U3A Memoir and Life Writing groups.

They are anecdotal recollections of incidents that occurred, and characters who lived in Mitchell almost 80 years ago. So, although they are true as far as I recall, there may be the odd inaccuracy. If you should find one, be a bit forgiving and put it down to a seriously senior lapse of memory.

I have changed a few names here and there. I'm not sure why. But I certainly don't want anyone to be offended or embarrassed by anything I've written.

Indeed, I hope only that you, the reader, will find some diversion in my recollections of a generally happy and carefree boyhood in Mitchell, Queensland where I was born.

A special thanks to my editor and publisher Lindy Bell, our tutor in both writing classes. Without her encouragement and generous assistance this modest but hopeful publication would never have come into your hands or mine.

THE MAN OF THE HOUSE

Our new neighbour, Mrs Mauritz, was a heavy, slow-moving woman. She was about sixty - though to my seven-year-old eyes and those of my four younger sisters she seemed very old indeed.

Her face was round and flat, with jowls like dumpy sausages lying along her bottom jaw, behind a round pink chin. Between this chin and a curiously sunken but active Adam's apple, two or three other chins hung loosely. I thought it was the heaviness of her face which caused her to speak so slowly. It was interesting to me that when her voice stopped, her face seemed to wobble on for a little while, as if it could not stop in time. Two other things fascinated me about Mrs Mauritz. First there were her glasses, so thick that her yellow-brown eyes looked like overcoat buttons. When she took her glasses off her eyes shrank magically. Then there was her hair. It was grey and remarkably long, although I was not to know how long until I started work. She wore her hair plaited in two big fat buns which covered her ears. I thought this probably explained why she so often said to Mum, 'I beg your pardon Mrs Welch. I'm getting hard of hearing these days.' She had some odd expressions.

Every night as Mum and I and the girls - the youngest always perched in the baby's highchair on Mum's right - sat at the kitchen table, Mrs Mauritz would appear at the back steps and greet us with the same surprise-filled question: 'Are you just dining?'

Mum always answered for us. It was just as well because to me it seemed a strange question indeed. Anyone could see we were having tea. Even later when I made the connection between the participle 'dining' - Mrs Mauritz was the only person I had met who used it - and the noun 'dinner' it still seemed a funny question. After all, dinner was what we ate in the middle of the day at our place. At school, for some strange reason probably connected with bells, it was called lunch. And even if you took 'dining' to mean 'eating' - Mum suggested that I should - it still seemed odd that Mrs Mauritz should always open the conversation with 'Are you just dining?' It was perfectly obvious that we were. In later years I suspected that it was her way of pretending to apologise for coming at what might fairly reasonably be considered an awkward time ... when in fact she timed her arrival to perfection so she could say, 'Well, if it's not too much bother,' when Mum, as she always did, offered her a cup of tea.

Those evening visits from Mrs Mauritz had become gradually more frequent during the three or four months that she and Arthur had been living in town. Before they moved to town they had lived for many years - I did not doubt that - on a little farm across the river. Now her Arthur had a job driving a truck for the Shire Council. It was this circumstance that directly led to my own start in the working world.

One night Mrs Mauritz engaged Mum in a very long and one-sided conversation about loneliness. My father was almost never home because he worked as a stockman on stations up to forty or fifty miles out of town. He rode in on a horse now and then for a few days, or perhaps even a week at showtime or Christmas. Mum had never discussed loneliness with us kids but then there were five of us around her all the time, so I suppose it never seemed necessary to bring it up. Anyway, it turned out that Mrs Mauritz was going to be lonely in the house at night because Arthur, her hubby - another one of her peculiar words I thought - would be camping out with the men for three or four weeks doing roadwork up the river.

To be honest, I felt a stab of genuine sympathy for her as I thought of her spending the long, dark winter nights by herself at "Clancy's". That's what we kids had called the long-empty, old, brown weatherboard house on the corner where the Mauritzs had recently come to live. No-one had ever lived in it before in my lifetime, but it belonged to a man called Brusher Clancy whom my dad sometimes talked about. The house was rather dilapidated, and before the Mauritzs moved in, the garden had run wild, so that the trellis-climbing roses and honeysuckle and the drooping pepperina trees seemed to enclose it in secrecy. The oleanders bordering the red gravel path reached branches towards each other, as if to bar entry, though the iron gate was unlatched and hung crookedly from a single, creaking, rusty hinge. Bringing our old milking cow home in the winter dusk, I always hurried past in the middle of the sandy lane which was Ann Street. A peculiar chill would creep up my neck as "Clancy's" aroused in me the feelings that I knew Jack - another boy responsible for the family cow - must have had as he ran for the beanstalk with the roaring giant getting closer all the time. Little did I know that "Clancy's" was to be the scene of the first test of my own manliness.

Before Mrs Mauritz left that night, my mother had agreed to allow me to stay with her on weeknights while her husband was away. Her Arthur would be home at weekends. Mrs Mauritz would collect me in the evenings and get me up at six-thirty in the mornings so I could get home for breakfast, do my few odd jobs and be off to school in good time.

To be fair, I must say that I had the chance to refuse. But I knew it would not have been neighbourly.

And I did not want to let on that I was frightened of "Clancy's". Mum had always said I was the 'man of the house' when Dad was away. I was always flattered by the idea and sometimes, when I was cutting chips at the woodheap with my tomahawk, or yarding the cow for milking, it almost felt possible that she could be right. I tried not to dwell too much on the responsibility of defending my mother and sleeping sisters against drunken or murderous intruders in the middle of the night. I had found that such thoughts kept me awake in the dark listening for creaking verandah floorboards. Or when I did eventually get to sleep, I would have horrible dreams from which I would awaken only a moment before death - and long after my speed of foot (my only resemblance to Jack apart from our work with cows) was embarrassingly obvious to Mum and the girls. They would have been disappointed in me in my dreams.

But luckily when I woke, they always seemed to be sleeping peacefully, so I knew they must have been having different dreams from me and I felt doubly relieved.

It occurred to me that now might be the time to say that I didn't like Mrs Mauritz much. Apart from the things I have mentioned - most of which I supposed she could not help - there were her eleven cats. I didn't like cats – except for Mrs Colville's Thompson. We had a little brown and white Kelpie Pomeranian watchdog called Darby. However, I decided that if I came out with all this criticism, it would only hurt Mrs Mauritz's feelings and embarrass Mum.

But perhaps I would not have agreed so meekly had it not been for the fact that it was to be a temporary arrangement - four weeks at the most her Arthur had said. There was also the shilling. Mrs Mauritz had looked me straight in the face with her honest, overcoat button eyes as she said, 'I will give Mervyn a new shilling on Friday each week he keeps me company.' In the bright warmth of our kitchen, I could almost see it shining in my hand.

But on the following Monday night I started reluctantly. Despite Mum's repeated hints that I needed a good night's sleep for school next day, Mrs Mauritz had stayed on and on. The girls were asleep in bed, and I sat drowsily waiting. At last Mum took the flat irons off the stove and folded the ironing blanket by way of showing that she was ready for bed. Mrs Mauritz shuffled to her feet and said, 'Well Mervyn, if you're ready, we best be off.' Mum kissed me and saw us down the steps with the lantern. She waited on the verandah 'til I closed the front gate behind us, then softly called a last 'Goodnight!'

It was pitch dark and icy cold. Mrs Mauritz said again as she had several times that evening: 'There'll be a white frost in the morning. I suppose the taps will be frozen again.'

'Yes, it's very nippy,' I said, in imitation of Mum.

I was glad Mrs Mauritz had a torch – a flashlight she called it – but it provided scant light that night.

'I think the batteries are about done Mervyn,' she said as we padded along towards the inky pepperinas lining "Clancy's" front fence.

It was not a long walk from our gate to hers – only about sixty yards – but it seemed a lot further in the dark. And Mrs Mauritz moved in a slow, deliberate waddle. In spite of my secret longing to back out of the whole thing, I found myself inching ahead of her. When we reached the gate, the oleanders lining the path looked more sinister than ever, and the house itself appeared to crouch in the blackness of the overhanging trees.

Inside the collar of my woollen dressing gown, I felt a familiar creeping cold.

I opened the iron gate and almost jumped as it creaked. I had the presence of mind to remember my manners and stood aside to let Mrs Mauritz go through. To my disappointment, she put her hand between my shoulder blades and gently pushed me ahead of her. She waited as I closed the gate and then, as I turned around, I got a sudden and terrible fright.

The cats' eyes were glaring at me. The creaking gate must have alerted them to our approach, and they were looking out at us from the blackness beneath the low, sprawling house. The sudden appearance of all those eyes glowing in the dark quite unnerved me, and I must have halted for a moment or perhaps I even took a step backwards.

Whatever I did, Mrs Mauritz must have thought it the right time to bring in some supernatural reinforcements. She did not go to any church and had not mentioned religion at all during the talk about my 'keeping her company'. My mother never talked about religion anyway because she said it was a person's own business and that God loved everyone - so I thought it a bit unfair when she suddenly came out with, 'You're a good Catholic Mervyn. You say your prayers so there's no need to be afraid. You go on ahead.'

She seemed to be putting me on the spot the way the soldiers had done, the three times to St Peter.

It occurred to me to remind her that she had the torch and if she went ahead, we might both be able to see where we were going, but I thought it would sound cheeky, so I just forced my shaky legs to go forward towards the cats' eyes. Before I reached the steps, I'd despatched half a dozen "Hail Marys" through the darkness towards heaven.

The pale glow of the torch jerked rhythmically along behind me, and Mrs Mauritz crooned greetings to Tibby and Thomas, Samson, and Susie. The cats had come out and were wheeling silently about her feet.

Once we gained the verandah Mrs Mauritz seemed to think we were fairly safe. She unlocked the front door and flashed the torch the length of the hallway.

I followed her into a mustiness that ever since I have associated with cats, old people and "Clancy's". She lit a kerosene lamp and carried it aloft as we inspected every room. Finally, we went into the kitchen where she took a brick out of the oven and wrapped it in a piece of grey flannel.

'This is how I keep my tootsies warm Mervyn,' she said. I wondered about mine.

I waited in the gloom of the hallway while she got ready, as she put it, 'to retire'. I guessed, correctly as it turned out, that she was getting ready for bed.

After what seemed a very long time she called, 'You can come in now Mervyn.' I opened the door and stepped timidly into the bedroom.

My employer was standing on the far side of the bed in a calico night-gown such as I had seen only in a picture book about Wee Willie Winkie. But other changes soon distracted me from the strangeness of her nightdress.

With her false teeth out, her lips fell loosely inwards, and she made whistling sounds when she spoke. Her eyes, without the glasses, were dewy beads. But the most startling change was her hair. Released from the plaited buns, it hung down her back in thick, grey ripples reaching almost to the back of her knees. I wondered if it made her head ache to carry all that weight around and I silently prayed that I wouldn't get tangled up in it during the night. Sometimes, after a night of bad dreams, I would wake with the sheets and blankets all twisted and tangled around me. I was just thinking about that when she said, 'I hope you don't kick Mervyn. I don't like to be woken once I go to sleep.'

When I was under the blankets on my side, Mrs Mauritz blew out the light. It was then that it occurred to me that I was closest to the door and if there was a burglar - at my age the word suggested murder rather than robbery - he was sure to grab me first. "Keeping company" had hidden depths of danger which I had not really anticipated.

I remembered the shilling and wished I hadn't been so greedy.

Mrs Mauritz huffed and wriggled down into the feather mattress and, sighing contentedly, settled her feet on the warm brick. I wriggled my toes and wondered if her Arthur always had cold feet too.

I was beginning to relax a little at last when Mrs Mauritz suddenly turned her face full on me and said: 'You're the man of the house Mervyn. If you hear any cats squalling in the night, it will be the Colvilles' Thompson interfering with my Tibby. Get up and shoo him off home.'

I wondered if I should remind her about Mum saying I needed a good night's sleep. Before I could decide she added, 'Good night, Mervyn. Don't forget to say your prayers.'

It was one time that I didn't need to be reminded. In the general 'God bless …' I cut the list down to Mum, Dad and the girls. I left out all my lucky cousins sleeping safely in their own beds. I even left out the soldiers in New Guinea who, like me, were in danger, but who had a lot of people praying for them. While I lay in the dark with Mrs Mauritz snoring - I had always known that old people did it - contentedly on her side, I silently repeated the Hail Mary. It seemed the best prayer for the situation, but I was careful to make a clear pause between 'now' and 'at the hour of our death' so that God's holy mother would know that I wanted her help now, but that I wanted to live a lot longer.

Eventually I fell into a dreamless sleep and the next thing I knew was being wakened by Mrs Mauritz tugging at my ear. 'Time to get up sleepy head,' she said in a tone which suggested that I was a bit of a disappointment to her. But it did not spoil my joyful relief that we had got safely through the night.

Things were never quite so difficult after that. But I always felt on Friday morning that a shilling was not an excessive sum to be paid for being the man of the house for Mrs Mauritz. And I had no real regrets when the four weeks were up and her Arthur, true to his word, came back to sleep with his wife on the side nearest the door.

PROBABLY NOT QUITE A MIRACLE

I was late home from school the afternoon before the cyclone hit Mitchell. I had played marbles for nearly an hour after school with a couple of classmates and a few bigger boys. We played on a hard, flat circle of ground near the front steps of our primary school – St Patrick's Convent.

Marbles was our game of choice at the time. It was a fad that came and went periodically throughout my seven years at St Pat's. Sometimes we played for fun, but mostly we played for keeps. That day Spank Rush, a skinny, sharp-faced boy a year or so older than I was, won most of the marbles off the rest of us. He was a wizard on "Knuckle down, screw-tight, fin-drawbacks" and, despite his frail build, had a powerful thumb flick that turned a marble into a missile.

Our school, a cream weatherboard building set on high stumps, comprised one large classroom in the centre, with two narrower, completely separate classrooms on either side of it. One of these 'end rooms" housed the infant classes – Preps 1 and 2 and Grades 1 and 2. In the big room in the middle were Grades 3, 4 and 5. And at the "top end" Sister Mary Godfrey, a sweet little Irish nun, taught grades 6 and 7.

I was in Grade 3 and probably 8 years old when the cyclone struck. My teacher that year was Sister Mary Justin, a plump, cheerful, rosy-cheeked nun who always had a little cluster of spittle bubbles at the corners of her mouth. I used to wonder if they were the same ones all day, or if she kept making new ones.

The front stairs of the school facing the front gate and Alice Street consisted of a single, wide panel of railed steps that reached from the verandah to about half-way to the ground. Then it branched into two somewhat narrower sets of steps that went to the ground on either side.

I used to think that those front stairs made the school look grand, much more impressive than the front stairs of most of the high-set houses in Mitchell, which had only a single row of stairs from the ground to the front door of the verandah.

As it happened though, we rarely used the front stairs – most of our outdoor activities being conducted in the sparsely-grassed playground at the back of the school. But, on the occasions that we were required to use the front stairs, the boys went down one side and the girls the other. The nuns were very particular about such formalities. At the time I thought it must have something to do with manners.

The architecture of St Patrick's Convent is relevant to my story only because of my brand-new, tiger-shooter helmet. It was grey with green lining under the brim and, being made of cork, was light as a feather. It had a strong elastic string in a sleeve at the base of the crown, which could be adjusted to the sort of snug fit you needed in a whirlwind, or when you were fairly flying down the hill over the railway crossing on your Malvern Star pushbike.

While we were playing marbles, I had put my helmet on one of the railing posts where the stairs divided on their way to the ground. That post must have been about as round as my head because I remember the helmet fitting quite snugly on its temporary perch.

When I got home, I got into trouble. Not so much for being late – I had afternoon chores to do, like bringing the wood and chips in for our wood stove and fetching our milking cow with her calf home from The Common for milking the next morning – but for leaving my brand-new, tiger-shooter helmet at school. And out in the open if you please!

I don't think we had any warning about the cyclone, "a significant weather event" in today's "all bases covered" weather forecast jargon. We got the local newspaper (The Mitchell News or the Maranoa News, I can't quite remember) - only once a week, on Saturday, and our wireless, a small bakelite His Master's Voice mantelpiece model, hardly ever worked properly and was never audible above the static on cloudy days.

Anyway, we had eaten tea - dinner was what we had in the middle of the day on weekends, whereas lunch was what we took in our bags to school - and having helped Mum with the dishes, I was in my pyjamas doing my homework when the wind suddenly strengthened.

Mum and I scurried around the house shutting doors and putting the windows down. Mum brought the budgerigar in from the verandah and set the cage on the kitchen table, with a towel over it. Under the table she made a bed for our little Pomeranian house dog, Darby.

In no time at all, it seemed, there came a terrifying roaring and whooshing sound, such as I'd never heard before, and things began to bang and rattle outside. Mum told my three younger sisters to get out of bed and, grabbing a couple of blankets and pillows from her own bed, she spread them out on the linoleum under the most solid piece of furniture we owned – the silky oak dining room table.

There the five of us huddled together for the next four hours – although it seemed like four nights – while our old brown weatherboard home shuddered and creaked as it was buffeted by the fiercest gale ever to blow into Mitchell. The rain, when it started, pelted our corrugated iron roof with deafening force and, although we were crammed tightly together under the table, Mum had to shout her assurances that we would be alright. And outside there was a constant banging and crashing as the tornado-like wind picked up anything moveable and hurled it with terrifying force against trees, fences and walls.

There was no chance that any of us, not even Myril, my baby sister, would fall asleep while the storm raged.

Eventually, towards midnight, the force of the wind lessened noticeably, and we knew the worst was over. And yes, as Mum had repeatedly promised, we were alright.

We were beginning to relax, and Mum was about to usher us off to our own beds when we were startled by a loud knock at the back door. A man shouted, 'Are you alright in there Mrs Welch?' It was George Vale, a friendly neighbour who lived a block away behind us. Knowing that Mum was on her own with us four kids, he had put on his wellington boots, and his khaki army overcoat over his pyjamas, and cut across our flooded back paddock to make sure we were safe.

I guess George Vale may have invented Neighbourhood Watch, though no-one had heard of it back then, so he didn't get the credit for it.

Before he left, he gave a bit of a laugh and remarked: 'Well, you've got some interesting ironing in front of you Mrs Welch.'

Next morning, Mum's first thought was for the cow and calf. We hurried outside and looked up the back towards the cow bail and there was Myrtle, our precious black and white milker, standing loyally and protectively beside the pen in which her calf was locked up every night.

And Mr Vale's joke took on its full meaning. Our single-wire clothesline, strung from posts at either end and on wash days supported in the middle by a straight pole - the clothes prop - was bedecked with buckled sheets of iron from roofs and sheds streets away - perhaps even the school - as I was soon to find out.

Although Mum was pretty sure there would be no school that day, we did not really know how much damage had been wrought in the town. I dressed in my school clothes, and after breakfast I rode my bike down to see what was happening. Some of the houses I passed had lost all or part of their roofs and there were branches and debris in every yard, and sheets of iron all over the road. A couple of pepperina trees had been uprooted and sprawled across the footpath and onto the road in Rugby Street.

When I got to the school, I was delighted to see a large sign on part of a blackboard leaning against the front fence. Printed in large, neat letters in red chalk it read "School Cancelled 'til Further Notice".

My heart leapt, but I immediately thought, 'No wonder!' The school was a disaster zone. The roof had been blown off, doors and windows had been blown in and smashed, and the grounds were strewn with broken bits of furniture and shredded books and maps. Debris was piled several feet high against the tennis court fence.

I parked my bike against the front fence and walked to the font stairs. Incredibly, my brand-new tiger-shooter helmet had somehow stuck to its post and, though completely ruined and drooping sadly, sat forlornly exactly where I had left it.

When school resumed a whole week later it was not in the school but in the old church where the Catholic youth held their fortnightly dances and the old folk played euchre on Friday nights.

I could hardly wait to ask Sister Mary Justin, 'Was it a miracle?' I meant about my helmet staying on the post, while so many bigger, heavier things were blown all over the town.

She smiled and said, 'Probably not quite a miracle.' But she must have seen the disappointment which I could not quite hide.

I had been thinking I might be famous, like those three kids in a place called Fatima in Portugal who had seen God's mother three times lately. Or those two boys who gave Jesus a tiny fish - probably a guppy - and a very small loaf, and then he fed 5000 starving people who had been following him around all morning in the hot sun while he made speeches.

Probably not wanting to hurt my feelings too much, she added that although it was 'probably not quite a miracle', it was an excellent example of the fact that 'God works in mysterious ways.'

I wasn't quite sure why, but somehow I felt somewhat consoled by the fact that God would bother to hold my helmet in place all through the raging cyclone when he must have been so busy dodging flying objects and trying to hold roofs on all over town.

MRS MARSHALL IS A SPY

After the cyclone, school was conducted in the "Old Church" – a weatherboard building at the side of the recently built and newly-consecrated St Columba's Church.

The old church looked a bit like an ugly sister beside its imposing replacement – the new and more modern St Columba's. It was barely adequate as accommodation for the whole school, but the nuns promised that we would be back in our real school "shortly". The Catholic carpenters, led by Jack Callow, four or five of whose children attended St Patrick's Convent at the time, would work both day and night to repair the damage inflicted by the cyclone. And so they did! Well, not all night but certainly into the dark. And in less than a month we were back in our almost good-as-new school.

It was while we were attending school in the old church that I made my unintentionally dramatic stage debut.

We were to have a concert in the Shire Hall as a gesture of gratitude to the carpenters, plumbers, painters and various other tradesmen and the many parent volunteers who had contributed to repairing our school.

Sister Mary Justin, our Year 3 teacher, decided that our class would perform a play entitled "Who Killed Cock

Robin?" You may not have heard of it as I don't think it was very famous. The good thing about it was that everyone in the class had a part to play.

The chorus line was the name of the play – "Who Killed Cock Robin?" - and the whole class, except the "suspect" of course, would call the question out at the appropriate - and sometimes an inappropriate moment - until we got the hang of it.

Cock Robin had the easiest part. Being dead, he just had to lie on the floor while the rest of us stood around him, looking suitably saddened by his "murderous demise".

Hughie O'Sullivan, a tubby, brown-eyed boy who bit his fingernails down to the quick and came to school barefoot most days, was Sister Justin's favourite. So of course, he was given the title role. One of the girls, Doreen Mahon – a pretty girl with two plaits as thick as hawser ropes, was chosen to read, and eventually recite, the narrative. The rest of us were assigned roles as Cock Robin's fellow creatures. There was a sheep, a cow, a donkey, a pig and various other characters. I was the crow.

Every day we would have a fifteen or twenty-minute rehearsal before we went out to lunch at 12:30. It was February, and a particularly hot summer in Mitchell. The old church was naturally pretty stuffy with the entire school population - probably about one hundred kids - crammed in together.

On the Wednesday of what was to be our last week in our make-shift school I unintentionally heightened the drama of our rehearsal. Whether it was the pressure of the approaching public performance to be staged on the following Friday night, or just the stifling heat that caused it I'm not sure.

But when it was my turn to deny culpability for the heinous crime - of killing Cock Robin - I had to say 'Caw, caw, not I," and the chorus would say, 'said the crow.' I got only one slow 'Caw' out before the second one trailed off into an elongated and unfinished 'ca-a-a-a' and I shocked my fellow thespians by keeling over on top of the hapless and already dead Cock Robin.

When I came to myself, probably in less than a minute, I found myself to be the centre of attention. Sister Mary Justin was kneeling over me looking very concerned and patting my cheeks, and the other animals - well my classmates, really - had shocked looks on their faces and were leaning in to see if I had replaced Cock Robin in the role of corpse - a real one perhaps.

Sister Mary Justin reached into the deep pockets of her voluminous black habit, took out her dainty white handkerchief with lace edging, and sent Geraldine Stein out to wet it under the tap, exhorting her to be as quick as a bolt of lightning. Hughie O'Sullivan had scrambled to his feet and had a puzzled look on his face. He clearly had not expected to be awakened so abruptly from his eternal rest.

When Geraldine came back with the dripping hanky, Sister took it and waved it vigorously in the air before laying it gently on my forehead. She told the animals - kids really - to 'Stand back and give him air." They moved back a bit reluctantly, but I don't think any of them gave me anything. How do you give air away anyway? I wondered.

When she thought I could safely sit up, Sister Mary Justin put one hand on the back of my neck and gently pulled me forward to touch my forehead to my knees. I thought it was a strange time to have me doing "drill", which is what we called PE in those days.

After a few "forward bends" Sister Mary Justin said I could stand up, and if I felt well enough, have a drink - Geraldine now held a glass of water out to me - and go home. I certainly felt much better straight away.

I walked out the gate with a Tom Sawyer spring in my step and a song of freedom in my heart. I had a whole afternoon off school! It was a wonderful and unexpected surprise and, combined with the attention I had commanded by my recent spectacular collapse, I felt I had achieved a happy status of considerable importance.

So I was unprepared for the put-down handed me by Mrs Marshall, whose house I passed on the way home. Some of the kids had been saying that Mrs Marshall might be a spy. The war was on and our enemy, the Japanese, had bombed Darwin and were marching down through New Guinea towards us.

There was an American Air Base in Charleville, some hundred miles to the west of Mitchell, and a US Army detachment had been based in our town for some months. Every house had an Air Raid Shelter and there was a large one in the school grounds.

At night, when we sat out on the lawn to escape the stifling heat inside, we would occasionally watch small planes - 'Tiger Moths if they are ours, probably,' Mum would say - flying either east or west with green or red lights blinking. Someone had seen Mrs Marshall in her front yard with a torch one night, and a rumour got around that she was signalling to a plane. Was it a Japanese warplane being flown by a kamikaze pilot, we kids wondered?

It would be safe to say there was something of a siege mentality developing in our town - especially among us kids. Mrs Marshall had a German name, and the Germans and the Japanese were on the same side - our enemies.

Anyway, Mrs Marshall was in the front yard playing the hose on some struggling geraniums as I walked jauntily past on my way to a half-holiday.

'What are you doing going home at this hour?' she asked abruptly.

'Sister sent me home,' I said, adding after a dramatic pause, 'because I took a fit.'

'You didn't take a fit,' she scoffed. 'What happened?'

'I did! I took a fit. I fell over and all.'

'That doesn't mean you took a fit you little scallywag!' she laughed. 'You probably just fainted.'

By this time, I was past her gate and would have had to

shout to continue the argument, which she seemed determined to win. So, I let her have the last word.

But when I got home, I got in the first word to my surprised mother. Before she could ask me why I was home before lunch time, and before I even took off my school bag, I burst out with 'Mrs Marshall probably is a spy.'

Mum looked shocked. 'What is going on? Why are you home? What has Mrs Marshall got to do with anything?'

So I told her. 'Mum, I took a fit. I fell right on top of Hughie O'Sullivan, and I didn't even know I did until Sister Mary Justin was patting my cheeks and looking very worried. Sister Mary Justin said I should come home. And Mrs Marshall said I didn't take a fit. I don't like her one bit.'

To my great disappointment Mum put her hand on my head and said, 'It was probably just the heat in that old building without a breath of air. You must have fainted, love.'

It seemed my own mother had joined the enemy!

MY CAREER TAKES OFF

I told you about my first job – sleeping with our neighbour's wife for a shilling a week. I wasn't sorry when Mrs Mauritz's husband, Arthur, came back to town and replaced me in her bed. From my point of view that first job was never going to be permanent. I think I told you it was too stressful anyway.

My second job came up quite unexpectedly and was a much more exciting opportunity.

On a Tuesday afternoon I was pedalling home on my too-big, black and green, fixed-wheel Malvern Star bicycle with a bag of groceries, meat and bread swinging from the handle-bars, when I met Mr Clive Henness, exercising two of his racehorses.

He was riding the big yellow bay with the blaze face and leading the flashy liver chestnut horse. I slowed right down as usual and veered as far away as I could on the road without going into the sand at the edge and probably toppling over. I knew that racehorses were highly strung and easily stirred up. Dad was a good horseman and he had taught me quite a lot about horses from when I was little.

'Got a minute Sparrow?' Mr Henness called, easing the

horses to a stand-still. So I pulled right up, and half fell off the bike as usual but, luckily, landed on my feet. I was pretty nimble, and I'd had a lot of practice.

'Well done!' said Mr Henness with a wide smile, 'That bike is a bit too big for you yet. But you'll grow into it soon enough for sure.'

That's what Mum says,' I answered, 'and she always points to my feet. I'm not sure why, but she says they point to the future. Some sort of sign.'

'Your mum is right about that,' he drawled. 'Look at the size of my riding boot.' With that he took his left foot out of the near-side stirrup iron and held it out towards me.

Straight away I thought there were kids at school whose shoes were bigger than Mr Henness' boots.

Mr (Clive) Henness had been a jockey in his younger days. He was still built that way – short and wiry – but he was too old to be a jockey anymore.

I realised then that if I were going to be a jockey, I would have to keep my feet small.

The horses, by now, were beginning to "mark time," clearly wanting to be on the move. So Mr Henness got to the point of 'Got a minute Sparrow?'

'Would you like to come and work for me?' he asked. 'Clive (the boy Parks had the same name as Mr Henness) will be fourteen in a couple of weeks. He'll be leaving school and going droving with his dad. I wondered if you'd like to take his place. I need another smart lad to help me with the horses. I've been watching you on that brown pony of yours, and you've got a nice seat and hands.'

'Thank you, Mr Henness,' I said. 'I would like to work for you. I love horses and I want to be a jockey when I grow up. But I'll have to ask Mum.'

'Of course you will,' he replied. 'It will only be on weekdays tell her. I have Bunyip Watson to help me on Saturdays, and on Sunday the horses have the day off. But you will need to be at the stables by 5 o'clock in the morning. I'll make sure you're home in good time to have breakfast and get ready for school. And I'll pay you ten shillings a week.'

I could hardly wait to get home and ask Mum; I was excited and quite "puffed up" by his praise for my riding. It seemed that this would be a great preparation for my career as a jockey. All I would have to do was keep my feet from getting too big.

Mum was a bit hesitant when I told her as soon as I got inside with the "messages." That was what we called the after-school shopping – "doing the messages."

I was relieved that none of the eggs were broken that day. Back then, when you bought eggs at the grocery store, they were individually wrapped in newspaper and put into a brown paper bag. Sometimes, especially when I rode Gertie - my brown pony with the star on her forehead - several eggs would be "scrambled" by the time I got home. The pony was always reluctant to go to the shops but coming home she would go "flat out" – making it impossible to hold the shopping bag still. When eggs were broken Mum would scrape what she could out of the paper bag and bake something with it. But she was never happy about it. It was a waste which we could ill afford.

'I don't know that you are ready for that sort of job Merv,' she said as she unpacked the groceries. 'Mr Henness is a gentleman, and it was nice of him to offer you that job. But you've got to keep up at school and it will be hard to get up and be at his stables by five in the morning.'

'I can do it Mum,' I replied eagerly, 'and I'll keep up at school, I promise.'

'Well, I'll think about it,' she said. 'But right now, you have to change and go and get Myrtle. It's getting late.'

I got out of my school clothes and put on my jodhpurs and work shirt and, after a glass of milk from the ice chest, and with a couple of Anzac biscuits in my shirt pocket, I headed out to catch and saddle my pony, Gertie.

I knew exactly where I would find Myrtle, our Friesian milker, and her month-old jet black bull calf. They would be over the river grazing on the green shoot that had appeared among the wilga trees after the recent showers.

Down the sandy lane past Symes's orchard, I urged Gertie into a fast canter and crouched low over her neck the way jockeys do. Already I was day-dreaming about galloping around the Mitchell racecourse on one of Mr Henness' big, shiny thoroughbreds.

Myrtle was right where I thought she'd be, and today she walked briskly and even broke into an occasional trot, as if she were looking forward to the biscuit of hay I always gave her once I'd penned the calf for the night.

Still, it was on sundown by the time I'd done that and let Gertie go.

I didn't ask Mum if she'd had enough time to think about the job when I got inside.

I checked the wood-box beside the stove and saw that it was pretty full. So I got my pyjamas and a clean singlet and went to have a shower and get ready for tea. Our shower was not in a bathroom. We didn't really have a bathroom.

What we had was a room beside the wash-house with a shower above a concrete floor which had a drain running out under the wall into the side garden. Mum always had a thriving clump of mint right there. Our bore water was always a bit warm, even in the depths of winter. And in summer it could get too hot to stand under after a couple of minutes.

After tea (that was what we called the evening meal) Mum washed up and I was drying the dishes when she suddenly said, 'We'll have to get an alarm clock then.'

I put my arms around her waist and hugged her with all my might. She ruffled my hair and added, 'But if it gets too much for you and you start to fall behind at school...' Before she could finish, I cut in with, 'I won't Mum, I promise.'

I'd already made up my mind to work even harder at school to keep a job I hadn't even started.

Mum bought the alarm clock at Short and Hobson's General Store – one of the two main grocery shops in Mitchell. It was the one where we shopped. We had a monthly account at Short and Hobson's and I knew all the staff and liked them. Jacky Hunter always had a joke with me, and I loved the way he kept his pencil behind his ear and snapped the string around his finger.

The brand of the clock was Westclox. It was a square, cream-coloured bedside model with a small alarm face high up on the dial, just below the twelve. You had to wind it up with a butterfly key when you set the alarm and pull up the button that you pressed down to stop the ringing when the alarm went off. Mum said I had to be quick at that so as not to wake up the girls who would be sleeping soundly at a quarter past four.

I started on my new job a week before Clive Parks finished up. Mr Henness said it would be good to have Clive show me the ropes. As it turned out, there were no "ropes" to show me – just routines to be followed and jobs to be done every day. Clive was good at his work, and I felt nervous about trying to take his place.

At ten minutes to five in the morning I would arrive at Mr Henness' house in Rugby Street with the stables out the back and park the Malvern Star inside the front fence. There would always be a promising plume of smoke climbing skywards from the kitchen chimney.

When I reached the top of the back stairs of the house I would smell the toast, and Mr Henness would drawl softly, 'Come in Sparrow.' He would be sitting on a chair in front of the wood stove with the fire box open. The teapot would be sitting on the side of the stove with steam coming from the spout and Mr Henness would be toasting a thick slice of bread (it was before sliced bread was thought of at the bakers') on a long toasting fork made neatly out of twisted fencing wire.

The kitchen was warm and welcoming, and Mr Henness toasted the bread properly on both sides and spread it generously with butter. He would put two spoonfuls of sugar in my milky tea. I thought it was a splendid way to start the day's work.

I loved these ten or fifteen minutes in the kitchen with my boss. We talked softly so as not to disturb Mrs Henness and their young daughter Kerrie whom he adored. It seemed that we had a sort of secret and special friendship which developed while the rest of the world was sleeping.

The stable work was fairly straightforward. Mr Henness would bridle the horse and lead it out to saddle it up while I picked up the night's droppings, raked up the bedding and emptied and refilled the water buckets.

Picking up the manure was the worst part. I had to pick it up by hand, put it on a triangular piece of hessian which Mr Henness used to cut from a used chaff bag, and carry it to the manure bay by the side gate. On Sundays people would buy it by the bag or trailer load for their gardens. I felt I was a secret contributor to vegetable and flower gardens all over the town.

I didn't mind picking up the night droppings. They were pretty dry by morning, had a fair coating of sawdust and not much by way of smell – something like a hint of tobacco. But the fresh droppings were a challenge – warm and steaming with a pungent aroma and so moist that they coated your hands a smeary yellow. It was nearly impossible to get rid of that odour on your hands no matter how hard you scrubbed in the clean-up water bucket with the bar of kerosene soap on the stump beside it. That was the only part of the job that I didn't like.

Once the horses were saddled, Mr Henness would leg me up on "Battle On" the big yellow bay that I had always admired and bring another horse, Valford the rangy chestnut, or the jet-black Broadway Bill for me to lead.

Then he would mount up and take another horse to lead and I would ride behind him along the sleeping streets and lanes to the racecourse on the outskirts of town. This was the part I loved best. I felt grown up – "doing a man's job" – and I wished more people were up and about and watching us ride past.

Sometimes Jim White, an old shearer who was a neighbour of ours, would be on the verandah in pyjamas and an old army overcoat smoking a cigarette in a holder. He would call out to Mr Henness, 'So you've got Todd Sloane with you today, Clive.' Todd Sloane was a champion American jockey – so that always gave me a surge of pride and pleasure.

Occasionally the horses would take fright at something – a zealous watch-dog charging the front gate or a ball of grass and weeds tumbling beside the road on a windy morning. I would have to hang on then – grip with my knees, swing on to the reins and sometimes grab a hank of mane while talking to the horses to settle them down.

Those times, Mr Henness would always say something encouraging. 'That was a good effort Sparrow,' or 'Darby Munro could not have done better than that.' Darby Munro was a famous Sydney jockey who won the Melbourne Cup on a horse called Russia. I would have worked for Mr Henness for nothing but those words of praise.

Dad rarely praised me, even when I thought I'd done something really well. Perhaps because when he was my age he was already droving with Mr Jim Burke. He was doing a man's job from the time he left school at the age of ten. But he probably didn't want me to get what grown-ups called "a swelled head" or get "too big for my boots." Mr Henness wasn't worried about those things – he just wanted me to know that he was pleased with how I'd handled a tricky situation. And that made me feel good.

I loved the time at the racecourse in the mornings – especially in the cold winter mornings – when it was still half-dark. The other trainers – Ted Reilly, Alec McKenzie, sometimes Giles Reilly and Peter Fuller – always spoke to me "man-to-man" in their kindly drawls.

Although I knew their first names, I always called them "Mr" and they called me Merv or "Young Punch." (Punch was my dad's name). They never called me "Sparrow." That was just between Mr Henness and me.

The first trainer to arrive at the track, usually Ted Reilly whose stables were only a stone's throw from the track, would light the fire in a four-gallon drum with slits in the sides and we would huddle around it to warm first our hands and then our backsides. I always felt pretty grown up among these men who, despite being excellent riders and skilled horsemen, showed no signs of having swelled heads and treated me as if I were one of them.

I began to feel that I had already commenced my career as a jockey. And I felt I was taking a big step forward when, after four or five weeks working for him, Mr Henness asked me if I would like to ride Battle On, the big bay horse, in his trackwork. I said I would love to do that. 'He can pull a bit,' he said, 'but he won't do anything wrong if you just sit on and let him bowl along. Anyway, don't panic if he gets away on you. Keep him on the rails and he'll pull up at the six furlongs where he always does.

And that's exactly what happened the first few mornings. Mr Henness gave me some riding tips on how to restrain him to a slower pace. 'Keep the bridge on his neck and turn your hands down from the wrist' he said. 'That way you'll keep his head down and you'll have more control.' That advice, and the fact that the horse got used to having me on his back on the track, helped a lot. I loved that morning track-work – especially when Mr Henness worked another horse, usually Valford, beside us. Even though we were only doing what Mr Henness called 'steady pace work,' I felt it was a bit like riding a race. I liked it especially when Battle On had his head in front of the other horse at the winning post – even though we weren't really racing. I was secretly imagining what it would be like when I began to win real races – in jockey colours and all – and the crowd cheering me.

It was while I was working for Mr Henness that Dad took a job as Head Stockman on Winneba Station about sixty miles north-west of Mitchell, and Mum went with him as Station Cook.

This meant that there were some serious changes in our family life. Only two of my sisters, Maureen and Lola, had started school, so they were put into the Convent as boarders. That's what most of the girls from Catholic Station families did during their primary school years – they boarded at the Convent with the nuns.

The nuns were strict and boarding at the Convent wasn't much fun. The girls had to get up early to attend Mass every morning. The big boys at school used to say, 'You can tell if a girl is a boarder by the bumps on her knees.' It was true that they spent a lot of time kneeling – and to make their lives even less pleasant the food was pretty terrible.

It turned out that I was much luckier than my sisters. Lily Carlyon, our neighbour at the back, offered to board me. Lily and Hec, her husband, had three daughters – two of whom by then were away at secondary school in Ipswich. Only their youngest, Fay, was still living at home and attending the State School. She was doing Scholarship, the last year of primary school, and would be going off to Ipswich Girls Grammar the next year. So, the Carlyons had some spare rooms and beds.

Lily Carlyon was a big woman with large, pendulous breasts, big brown eyes, and a thick bottom lip. She liked a beer or two of an afternoon, a scotch before tea, and sometimes, another one or two before bed.

Lily was a smoker, too. She smoked Craven A tailor-mades, or she rolled her own with Havelock Fine Cut tobacco and Tally Ho cigarette papers. She would often have a roll-your-own dumper stuck on her bottom lip and wonder of wonders to me, she could talk while she was washing up or sweeping, not quite bringing her lips together, and that cigarette butt would wobble with every word – but I never saw it fall off.

There were hardly any cars in Mitchell back then. Only a few of the better-off people had a car and only the men drove them. The Carlyons did not own a car, but Lily had a Driver's Licence. She was the first woman in Mitchell to hold a Licence, and she was very proud of that. I wasn't sure how or why she got her licence, but I supposed it might come in handy someday.

Lily Carlyon was a kind woman and good to me in a rough and ready way. She was not my mum after all. There was always plenty to eat – plain food like porridge and toast for breakfast and a hearty meal of meat and vegetables for tea. Sometimes though, I had jam sandwiches for lunch at school, something Mum would never let happen. Mum would sometimes give me peanut paste sandwiches, but never jam. She couldn't tolerate the idea of my eating soggy sandwiches for lunch.

Lily wasn't a fussy ironer, either. Sometimes I felt a bit embarrassed going off to school in a shirt that looked as if I'd just taken it off the clothesline.

But from time to time a shearer named Gordon Kieran would stay at the Carlyons' between stints in the shearing sheds on the many sheep stations around Mitchell. Gordon was a tall, good-looking bachelor in his thirties and, unlike many of the knock-about men who made Mitchell home, he was very particular about his appearance. He taught me the basics of ironing, and he let me into one of his secrets. He showed me that, by pulling the damp edge of a worn-thin cake of soap along the underside of the crease in a trouser leg, the crease would not only look sharper, but would last longer.

When Gordon was in town, he would often do the ironing for Lily. My school clothes, and even my work clothes looked pretty smart then. Anyway, after those ironing tips I was able to give my clothes a rub-over if they needed it. At times like that I missed Mum – and being at home.

Otherwise though, my life went on as before. Mum and Dad had loaned Myrtle, our house cow, to the Carlyons. That probably helped with the cost of their boarding me because now they didn't have to buy that quart of milk each day from Arthur Fuller's horse-drawn milk-cart. Mr Fuller had a dairy out past the hospital, and he did a milk-run in the town on weekdays. My afternoon routine – doing the messages down town, filling the wood-box, and fetching the cow home from The Common and penning the calf for the night stayed the same.

And of course, I had the Westclox to wake me in the mornings to get me to Mr Henness' stables in good time. That brings me to the most exciting thing that happened during my time with Mr Henness. The time he took me with him to the Charleville races. When he asked me if I would like to go, he explained that I would miss three days of school – from Wednesday to Friday. That sounded wonderful to me, but Mr Henness said 'That's a fair bit of school to miss Sparrow. You'll have to ask your mother as well as Mrs Carlyon.'

So Lily rang Mum on the Friday night of the week before the races in Charleville. Lily and Hec had one of those wall phones that you had to stand up to. The speaker stuck out in front and the receiver hung on a hook on the side of the box. You wound the handle to ring the telephone exchange at the Post Office and asked the girl to connect you to the phone number of the person you wanted to speak to. She would then "put you through" on what was called a "party line," which meant that the girl at the exchange as well as everyone connected to that telephone line could "listen in" to what was being said if they wanted to.

The station manager answered the phone and I heard Lily ask if she could speak to Mum. When Mum came on the other end of the phone line Lily chatted with her for a few minutes, but she didn't mention the Charleville thing. She had told me before that I had to do it for myself.

When I told Mum about Mr Henness' offer and how much school I would miss, she asked if we were doing anything special at school – tests or exams that I shouldn't miss. I answered that it was only ordinary schoolwork that I'd be missing. She said I could go.

'Get a new white shirt at Short and Hobson's and take your best school shirt and pants. You will need to take clean underwear, your toiletries and shoe polish, and a towel. Ask Lily to check your port to make sure you've got everything and don't forget your manners. Don't let Mr Henness down.'

'Gee, thanks Mum,' I said, 'don't worry – I'll make him proud of me.'

Next morning, I rode my bike to Mr Henness' place to tell him that I could go. He was just having smoko, so he invited me to join him in a cup of tea and a scone with jam and cream. It tasted so good – especially as, while we were eating, Mr Henness outlined the plans for the trip.

On the Tuesday night I would have tea with Mr and Mrs Henness because we had to have the horses loaded on the 9 o'clock train. Mr Bill McKay, Mr Henness' main owner, would take our ports to the train, along with the feed we would need for the first day. We would have to buy the rest of their feed from the Feed Merchant in Charleville. It sounded like an exciting, grown-up adventure that I was about to have.

Even though I felt like telling everyone, I kept it a secret. I didn't want my very strict teacher, Sister Mary Catherine, to have a chance to get in some premature punishment to discourage me from going. I was already dreading returning to school on the Monday after the races, but I didn't dwell on it.

I don't think I had ever been so excited as I was when we loaded the horses Battle On and Valford onto the Half-

I-C-wagon that Mr Henness had booked well in advance. That afternoon he had taken some bales of straw and spread them about a foot deep on the floor to make the trip easier on the horses' legs. Both horses had travelled by train before, so they loaded easily but their eyes were everywhere, and their snorting showed that they were excited and nervous too.

I don't remember much about the train trip itself. I was dog-tired. Mr Henness had put in a swag roll for me, and I stretched out comfortably on the long seat. With the rocking of the train and the regular rattle of the wheels I was soon asleep.

Next thing I knew, Mr Henness was lifting the blanket gently from over my head saying, 'Time to wake up Sparrow, we are coming into Charleville,'

I sat up and looked out the window at the houses on the outskirts of town and felt as if I were entering a new world.

Mr Bill McKay met us at the train and took charge of our ports, swag rolls and the horse feed, telling Mr Henness that he would catch up with us later.

We unloaded the horses on the end of the railway platform, and they looked around as if they too were entering a new world. We led them along unfamiliar, but thankfully still deserted streets to the stables at Mr Billy Lambert's house. That was to be our "headquarters" while we were in Charleville, Mr Henness told me as we walked the horses.

The Lamberts' house was like Lily and Hec's, my now home in Mitchell. It was on high stumps and was concreted underneath with a shower in one corner. We slept downstairs, under the house. Mr Henness had a three-quarter iron bedstead, and I had a camp stretcher. We had plenty of blankets and soft pillows. It was very comfortable really.

Mr Billy Lambert was a bookmaker – which meant he stood up on a stool at the races with a big bag slung from his neck with his name on it. You could bet on a horse with him, and he would write you a ticket – like a receipt to show you had bet with him. Lots of other people would place bets with him on the same race so you needed to hold on to your ticket and present it to Mr Lambert if your horse won. In that case, he had to give you your money back plus some of his own. But if your horse lost, you might as well tear up your ticket because Mr Lambert would just keep your money. Anyway, he was a friendly man with rosy cheeks and tiny purple veins running all over them. He was not much taller than Mr Henness, but he was a lot heavier because he had a large stomach.

Mrs Lambert was a short, plump lady with twinkling blue eyes, grey permed hair, and chubby little hands. She always wore an apron – whatever she was doing. She was a good cook. We had bacon and eggs for breakfast, cold corned meat and salad for lunch, and steak, chops or sausages and onion gravy for tea. There were vegetables too for tea and always pudding – steamed syrup pudding with custard, or apple pie and ice-cream. I felt it was like staying at Buckingham Palace – though I hardly knew anything about the Palace except that the King and Queen lived there. So I supposed the food there would be pretty good.

The Lamberts didn't seem to have any children – perhaps they were too old – so Mrs Lambert made quite a fuss over me. They probably didn't have ten-year-old boys staying with them for the races very often. I dried the dishes for her as I used to do at home, and at Lily's, and she chatted to me all the time and thanked me when we finished. It made me feel "at home."

The Charleville trip was certainly the most grown-up experience I'd ever had. After tea Mr Lambert, Mr Henness and I would go down town and meet Mr McKay and the four of us would walk around for a while. Then we would go to Londy's Café where Mr McKay would order tea and toast for all of us. We sat in what Mr Henness called an alcove. It had a polished rectangular table screwed down in the centre with an upholstered bench seat on either side. There were partitions separating it from the next alcove, so it was a bit like having a small room to ourselves.

The tea and toast were brought to the table by a waitress wearing a sort of bonnet and a frilly apron. The teapot was silver and so were the milk jug and sugar basin. The toast, on a long silver tray, was cut into long fingers. There was plenty of butter on it and my mouth was watering at the sight of it. But I remembered what Mum had said about my manners and waited to be offered before I took my first delicious slice. It felt very special to be there with the three men when most kids my age would be in bed.

On the Thursday afternoon Mr Henness took me with him up the main street to do some shopping. He wanted to take something home for his wife and daughter. He picked out a navy and green silk scarf for Mrs Henness and he asked me if it was a good choice. I said it was nice, so he bought that and a pair of nylon stockings. For his daughter, who was probably three years old, he bought a doll with four faces. Under the doll's bonnet was a cork which you turned to change the face. Mr Henness said that Kerrie would be "tickled pink" when she opened the box that the shop lady put it in on a bed of pale blue tissue paper.

I had two pounds of my own, and Mr Henness suggested that I should take something home for Mum and the girls. He gave me one pound to add to my own spending money. I bought the girls each two handkerchiefs in a box with a clear cellophane lid. You could see the white handkerchief embroidered with a flower in the corner and edged with lace. For Mum I bought a pair of maroon felt slippers lined with fake wool. For Dad I got a packet of Log Cabin Fine Cut tobacco. That and Havelock were his favourite smokes.

We did not have much success at the races unfortunately. Though Mr Henness said the horses had 'done their best and pulled up alright,' so he was satisfied. The jockey said that they both 'needed a bit further.' But Mr Henness told me on the quiet that jockeys nearly always say that. I thought he should know because he had been a jockey himself in his younger days.

I forget to mention that Battle On ran fourth on both days, and Valford ran fifth on Friday, but third on the Saturday. That meant that we won a little bit on the tote for one race anyway.

Speaking of money, Mr Henness had promised to show me "a lot of money" before we went back to Mitchell. That happened on the Saturday night. After T-bone steak with onion gravy and vegetables, and pudding of apple pie and ice-cream, Mr Henness told Mrs Lambert that the meal made us feel like winners anyway. She blushed and said, 'It's a pleasure to cook for such perfect guests.' I wished Mum could have heard that.

Well, after I'd dried the dishes for Mrs Lambert, we left her listening to Bob Dyer on the radio and walked along some back streets, 'til we came to a big house set back from the road. There were lights on in the house and we could hear women talking and laughing and Bing Crosby singing Galway Bay on the gramophone.

It turned out that we were not going to the house. From the little gate at the corner of the front yard, we followed a neat, gravel path to a big shed at the back. As we got closer, we could hear the buzz of men's voices. Inside was a big group of men, most of whom were still in the clothes they had on at the races. Most were standing around a big table at which there were probably a dozen men sitting. At one end they were playing cards and at the other they were rolling dice. There was a heavy smoke haze in the air, and some of the gamblers were smoking cigars.

Mr Henness had told me we were going to a "school,"

but this was nothing like St Patrick's Convent which I attended. It was the first time I had seen money rolled up in rubber bands. They were fat rolls of ten- and twenty-pound notes – 'Probably a thousand pounds in some,' Mr Henness said on the way home.

It was just after the war and wool prices were sky-high. Wool was bringing one pound for a pound of wool, so the graziers were "rolling in money" driving Mercedes sedans and buying thoroughbred yearlings at sales in Brisbane and even Sydney.

Most of the gamblers were squatters or bookmakers. One of the biggest bettors was a man called Charlie Moxham. I recognised him from the races where he was the busiest bookmaker. He offered slightly longer odds than most of the others so there was always a queue of punters waiting to bet with him.

'Bookmakers rarely lose,' Mr Henness said on the way back to the Lamberts', 'If they are clever enough, they can make the book so that they win, even if the favourite gets up,' he added.

To be truthful I was finding it hard to concentrate on his explanation. I was already feeling a bit sad that the Charleville Adventure was almost over. This was the last time we would be going back to sleep at our "home away from home" under the Lamberts' house.

A couple of things I remember though. One was the full name of the place where we'd been. It was called a "Gaming School" or "Gambling School." I thought that I would be the only kid at our school who knew that meaning of the word "school." The rest of the kids in my class would only know about our kind of school or, the smarter ones, a school of fish as well. Mr Henness said he didn't know who thought up the name, or why.

But he said he hoped I'd learned something from watching what happened with gambling. 'Some of those men saw their money lost more than once tonight,' he said. 'They lost it themselves, but then the chaps who had won it ended up losing it too.'

'Don't ever take it up Sparrow,' he added. 'I never knew a gambler who didn't end up broke.'

Anyway, it had been an interesting, grown-up sort of experience for me. I felt a bit smug about it in fact. I knew that none of my mates at school would have seen anything like it.

But the word "school" and the thought of returning to mine had a dampening effect on me. It was hard to get Monday morning out of my head before I finally fell asleep in the camp stretcher under the Lamberts' house. But Monday morning turned out to be another story altogether.

THE LIE THAT GALLOPED AWAY

It happened when Mum and Dad were working on Winneba Station, and I was boarding in town with Lily Carlyon so I could attend school at St Patrick's Convent. I was reluctant to get up, even when Lily, my substitute mum, pulled back the blankets saying, 'Come on! I can't let you sleep in any longer. You'll have to get a go on, or you'll be late for school.'

She meant, of course that I had to shower, dress and have some breakfast before heading off to school.

But I had no appetite for anything, especially school. I would have gladly pulled the blankets back over my head, stayed in bed and gone without breakfast, lunch and even tea - which is what we called the evening meal back then - rather than face the ire of Sister Mary Katherine. She would be furious that I had taken three days off school to go to the Charleville races with Mr Henness and his horses.

That Mum had given me permission to go would not count at all with "Kate", which we kids irreverently called the old terror when out of carshot. She, and indeed all the nuns, regarded the racecourse as an "occasion of sin", where men gambled on horses with money that would

39

have been better put on the plate at the Sunday Mass collection.

That was one thing that puzzled me in Grade 5 - perhaps a hint of a double-standard on "Kate's" part. I don't know if I mentioned it before in another story, but her pet in our class was Hughie O'Sullivan. Hughie, or "Eugene" as "Kate" always called him when giving him important jobs like cleaning the blackboard or handing out the copybooks, was the son of an SP bookmaker affectionately known as the "Irish giant". The "giant" was no more than 5 foot 2 inches with his shoes on.

"Kate" obviously didn't hold the father's occupation as an illegal off-course bookmaker against his son "Eugene". But it was also true that the "giant" was one of the town's leading Catholics and never missed Sunday Mass. It is probable that he put some of his winnings from the town's leading mug punters on the plate, all of which would have earned him some redemption in the opinion of the nuns.

Anyway, on the Monday after the Charleville races I was filled with dread at the prospect of facing Sister Mary Katherine. In my mind I could see the fierce darkness in her eyes, the thin-set line of her mouth, and hear her wheezing breath as she gave me the full force of the ruler, first on my hands, then on my bare calves. I would have had to pull my long grey school socks down to my ankles.

With these thoughts filling my head I could hardly eat even half of the rolled oats porridge, and however much I chewed on the toast, it seemed too bulky and dry to swallow. My throat felt dry and seemed to have narrowed, so that each swallow had the sensation of an internal gravel rash.

Lily noticed my dawdling over breakfast - I was really trying to slow the clock down - and told me brusquely to 'Eat up, and hurry to brush your teeth. You're going to be late at this rate!'

Eventually I had to put on my schoolbag - it was one of those you wore on your back, held in place by two straps over the shoulders. 'Why does it feel so heavy today?' I thought, as I put on my school hat and headed down the path to the front gate. My legs felt as if I had been walking all night and it was an effort to pick up my feet and keep moving forward. I might have been walking to the gallows like poor, old Ned Kelly with the hangman waiting, noose at the ready and the trapdoor set for release.

Vera Vale, the freckle-faced girl who lived across the road, called out her usual cheery 'G'Day'. I managed to call 'G'Day' back in a voice that didn't even sound like me. It was oddly thin and squeaky. I thought again, maybe my throat has shrunk. Perhaps there is something wrong with me – maybe I'm getting very sick. And I hoped I was and that it was one of those sudden illnesses which get serious quickly – like in about the time it took me to walk to school.

When Vera called out 'G'Day' again I did not respond. She was a funny kid! She would call out 'G'Day' as long as she could hear you say 'G'Day' back. I counted the number of times she did it most mornings – the record was twenty-two – but today my heart was not in it. And today I stopped responding 'G'Day' on number two. I felt a bit sorry for her, but then I thought, 'It's alright for you Vera, you can say G'Day and go and play with your dolls.' She was only three or four and so hadn't started school, so hers was a trouble-free life.

It was a fine, sunny morning and Mrs Gibson's goats were frisking about in the spare allotment beside her house as I plodded along the footpath. Normally they would have lifted my spirits, but today my heart was too heavy.

By the time I reached Mrs Marshall's place – she was the woman most of us kids thought was spying for the Germans in the war – I knew I couldn't face "Kate".

I'd made up my mind to try for a postponement of the ordeal by pretending I was sick. I thought, 'Perhaps if I pretend hard enough, it might really happen.'

Anyway, I turned around and headed back home –

holding a hand on my stomach and staggering a bit every now and then in case anyone saw me going the wrong way and looking perfectly healthy.

When I got home Lily's greeting was about as friendly as Sister Mary Katherine's would have been. 'What are you doing back here?' she said. 'You should be at school by now.'

'I feel sick,' I said, which wasn't really a lie – but then I added, 'I've got a pain in the stomach,' which was a real lie.

'If you're too sick to go to school, I'm going to call the ambulance,' she blustered. 'Take your shoes off and get up on that bed!'

It was a high, three-quarter iron bedstead on the verandah. As I unlaced my shoes with fingers that felt strangely thick and stiff, I said 'Lily, I'm feeling a bit better. I think I'll be alright by tomorrow.'

But she was having none of that. 'No, if you're so sick that you can't go to school today, I'm calling the ambulance,' and with that she turned on her heel, marched back into the lounge room and took down the receiver from the black bakelite phone on the wall.

I could hear the whirring of the dial wheel and then I heard her voice. 'Hello Mr Holcombe, it's Lily Carlyon speaking. I wonder if you could come and have a look at a sick boy? He started off to school but came back complaining of a pain in the stomach.' There was a pause, then 'Thank you.' Another pause, and then, 'No, just when you have time. He's been away at the Charleville races and may have picked something up.' Again, a pause, then Lily said 'Yes, I'll keep him lying down. Thank you, Goodbye.'

Things had taken a whole new direction that I hadn't anticipated. It seemed I was no longer in control. And I suddenly wished I hadn't embellished the lie by adding the bit about the pain in the stomach to the much safer 'I feel sick.'

Now I began desperately trying to remember on which side of the stomach my appendix was located. Dr Williams, the local doctor, had the reputation of being a very good surgeon. And he should have been! He had lots of practice. It was a well-known fact that very few Mitchell kids reached puberty with their tonsils, adenoids and appendix still inside them.

Mitchell women did their washing on Mondays and their ironing on Thursdays. Dr Williams operated on the same days. And even if the women missed on either day, because of rain, or more likely a dust-storm, the "Doc" or the "Quack" as he was sometimes disrespectfully referred to, operated on schedule, whatever the weather conditions.

So now my fear was transferred and elevated to a new level. And I suppose I was in something of a panic as I tried desperately to recall where someone - I could not even remember who - had told me my appendix was. I needed to tell Mr Holcombe, the ambulance man, when he came, that the pain was on the other side. Of course, if I should hazard a guess, I would have a fifty-fifty chance of being right. But if I got it wrong, the consequences were too terrible to contemplate. And I remembered Mr Henness' warnings against gambling.

I was in a state of what could be called "extreme anxiety" when I heard the ambulance - the big yellow van with the red Maltese Cross on the sides and back - pull up at the front gate.

Shortly after there was the familiar squeak of the gate hinge and I knew that the old Dutchman, Mr John Holcombe, in his ambulance uniform - white shirt with button-down lapels, black trousers and peaked cap - was on his way to check me over. It felt like he was going to arrest me as he clomped heavily up the stairs to where Lily was waiting on the verandah to meet him.

He greeted Lily and she thanked him for coming so soon. 'I don't think it's anything serious,' she said. I didn't know whether it meant she thought I probably wasn't sick at all - which was of course true - but then she would have been saying I was probably putting it on or making it up.

So I wasn't sure whether I should be relieved or insulted.

'Best to have a look at him anyway,' Mr Holcombe said, in his harsh, croaky voice. And, walking over to the bed, he put his Gladstone bag on the foot of the bed and drew the blanket back to my knees.

'What seems to be the matter, young fellow?' he rasped as he put one hand flat on my forehead.

'I was feeling sick before,' I said, 'but I'm feeling better now. I think I'll be alright by this afternoon.' I didn't mention the stomach-ache, and I hoped he'd forgotten that Lily had mentioned it.

'Best to be sure,' he said, inserting a thermometer under my tongue and advising me not to bite on it. Then he took hold of my wrist and "listened to it" with his fingers.

When he took the thermometer out of my mouth and checked it, he announced 'Temperature's normal anyway.' I knew it would be normal of course, but I felt a momentary surge of hope when he said it.

'What's this about a stomach-ache?' he asked abruptly. 'Mrs Carlyon said you were complaining of a pain in the stomach.' The flicker of hope instantly died, but terror stimulated my brain. I suddenly knew what I had to say to avoid the possibility of unintentionally identifying the correct location of my appendix – with the possibly dreadful consequences.

'It was kind of all over.' I lied almost cheerfully – because of the relief I felt at my cleverness. 'But it's gone now, and I feel much better'.

Obviously a sceptic, he began prodding my abdomen in various places and each time he poked me he rasped, 'That hurting? Sore there?'

To which I answered most emphatically 'No!' I wanted him to know I was completely cured - even before the "laying on of hands".

After all those denials regarding discomfort in my stomach I was beginning to feel much more relaxed and to think that I had passed the medical test. I fully expected him to say 'Probably just an upset tummy. Let him rest for a while and he should be alright.'

So, I was shocked and horrified when he turned to Lily and said, 'Better let the Doc have a look at him. I'll take him up to the hospital.'

I thought very briefly of "owning up" - admitting that I had lied about being sick - having a pain in the stomach - and that it was a ruse to get out of facing Sister Mary Katherine.

But although at the time I could not have named my offence as being a "public nuisance" - I knew that having the ambulance come to the house for no reason was not merely embarrassing but probably deserving of attention by Sergeant Bergen – the burly and very severe policeman who struck fear into the hearts of even the toughest big kids who wagged school at both the Convent and the State School.

So, biting my lip and secretly hoping and praying that Mr Holcombe would suddenly be struck down as a healthy cripple unable to drive - or that Dr Williams had this very morning developed the shakes, like old Pirie Pickup - who, as he walked, did a twitchy kind of dance named after some Saint whose name I couldn't remember - and was no longer able to operate - so that I would have some breathing space to get Lily to bring up some holy water so I could be "miraculously cured" like the sick and crippled at Lourdes in France, I allowed the ambulance man to guide me gently -with a firm hold on my shirt - down the stairs and out to the big yellow van with the red Maltese Cross on the side.

Mr Holcombe asked me gruffly if I could sit up in the front seat beside him, or if I needed to lie down on the stretcher in the back of the van. I wondered about his intelligence - or was it his memory? Hadn't I just told him that the pain had gone, and I felt much better?

So, I decided to persist with the healthy line and said,

'I'll be right sitting up - because I feel quite well now.'

I was hoping he might finally realise the stupidity of taking a perfectly healthy kid up to the hospital and set me free at the last moment - perhaps calling out a word of warning to Lily, watching from the top of the stairs, to 'Keep an eye on him for the next few days.'

But it didn't work, and to my growing terror he closed the passenger-side door with a thud of finality and hurried around to the driver's side, as if he sensed I was thinking about making a dash for freedom - which of course I was.

Sadly, the motor started up first go. After doing a U-turn in front of Number 4 Alice Street, which is where I already thought I *used* to live, he headed down town past the church and the school - where even the kids in Sister Mary Katherine's class were safer and happier than I was. Then, over the hump at the railway crossing, across Cambridge Street - the main street of Mitchell - where the pensioners were already sitting yarning under the bottle tree outside Gunther's Newsagency, and then on out past the Showgrounds. We crossed over the bridge at the One Mile, arriving all too soon at the sprawling, weatherboard building that was, as the sign over the gate announced, the Mitchell and District Hospital.

I hadn't heard of the French Revolution by Grade 5, but years later when we did Modern History at boarding school, I recognised the feeling I had on that drive. It was what the trembling French nobles would have felt in the tumbrils on the way to the guillotine. The only difference was that the rest of the town on this bright Monday morning were not out jeering and throwing rotten fruit and eggs at us, the way the peasants did to the nobles as they passed along the streets of Paris.

By the time my uniformed captor had escorted me into the casualty room, still holding on to my shirtsleeve, I must have been pale with terror because grouchy old Sister Daly felt my forehead and announced: 'You are not well boy,' and hurried over to the basin in the corner to get me a drink of water.

I suspected she was in cahoots with Dr Williams and was determined to keep me captive.

I am not sure if it was that suspicion, her brusque manner or the peculiar antiseptic smell of the room, but by now I was so scared that I had trouble swallowing. The water seemed to baulk at my Adam's apple, give an audible glug and a bit of a flip before it went hurtling on its way to my nether regions.

Once he handed me over to the hospital with the report that I had been "experiencing stomach pains" - which was only a "white lie" because he didn't really know the truth, which was in fact a "proper lie" - he stalked off to the van and drove to the ambulance depot, no doubt to wait for the next "emergency" phone call.

I knew then that I had slid further into the abyss which I had unintentionally created because of my cowardice.

If I hadn't been acutely conscious of the cold vinyl couch under me and the antiseptic smell of the place, I would not have believed that my life had spiralled so out of control in just a few short hours. The unanticipated series of events that had landed me in this terrifying situation might have just been a pre-dawn nightmare, now devoutly to be wished.

The only good thing that happened in the doomed hours as I waited for Dr Williams to have a look at me was the vision of Sister Gillespie. Mum used to say she was the most beautiful woman in town and that most of the men in town - except Dad I supposed - were in love with her.

She came to the high counter in the casualty room to write something on a card, and when she saw me, she smiled and said, 'You're Punch Welch's boy aren't you?' I said I was, and she said, 'Steve tells me you are a very good rider, and that you'll be a champion jockey one day.'

Her brother Steve, who was a good bit older than she was, owned racehorses and had seen me on the track with Mr Henness quite a few times.

That compliment, and her lovely smiling face were a short-lived relief; but when she walked out before I could tell her I really wasn't sick, I felt more abandoned and alone than ever.

Not long after that, Dr Williams and the tiny Matron Frawley came in. The doctor was a big, burly man with greying hair and a close-cropped moustache, and he looked a giant beside Matron Frawley. I was appalled to see that he was still wearing his white operating gown and that there were several spots of blood on it.

'Someone must have spurted and splashed on him when he put the knife in,' I thought in horror.

His operating mask was hanging loosely from the string around his neck. He looked pretty scruffy for a doctor. And, with the blood on his gown, more like Tibby Blair, the butcher, by closing time.

'What are you doing here?' he asked in a very gruff voice - as if he had just found me trespassing on the hospital premises. Before I could say, 'I really shouldn't be here. I'm okay now,' Sister Daly bustled in and huffed, 'He's had severe stomach pains.'

Of course, she didn't know she was lying. Worse still, Dr Williams didn't know either, because he turned to little Matron Frawley and said, 'Keep him under observation and I'll do him on Thursday.'

I thought, 'If they don't keep me under observation I won't be here on Thursday.' But in my heart, I knew I wouldn't be game enough to take off and hide in the bush – just as I hadn't been game enough to face Sister Mary Katherine.

Of course, it was grumpy old Sister Daly who took me around to the male ward. I would have much preferred the lovely Sister Gillespie to be walking beside me, but I knew that everything was going wrong for me since I told the lie about being sick.

As she deposited me on the end bed in the almost-empty male ward, Sister Daly announced, surprisingly cheerfully I thought, 'You've missed lunch. I'll bring you a sandwich later when I get time. Take off your shoes and socks. I'll bring you a pair of hospital pyjamas and you can change in the bathroom.'

As I lay miserably in the end bed in the grey hospital pyjamas waiting what seemed ages for the promised sandwich, I wondered if I were actually responsible for all the lies that had been told that morning. I had obviously started them off, but Mr Holcombe and Sister Daly had kept them going even after I'd done my best to undo the first one by saying I was alright.

Would I have to remember them all and declare them to Father Flynn the next time I went to confession - if I ever got the chance?

Perhaps those other lies came under the heading of "being an occasion of sin for others." In that case I would certainly be the guilty one and Father Flynn would be obliged to give me a long penance - probably five decades of the Rosary - even though I was a good altar boy and he'd told the bishop that one day I'll be the Archbishop of Shanghai. That is a big city in China.

Anyway, all of that would probably not be happening now because it seemed to belong to another world in another time.

My lying had completely changed the course of my life.

Lily came up to see me that night. You could have visitors between 7pm and 8pm. She didn't stay for the full hour. It felt as if she had washed her hands of me – the way Pontius Pilate did when the people insisted on crucifying Jesus. She may have felt guilty about letting me get sick. Lily said that she had rung the manager at Winneba Station and that Mum and Dad would be coming to town tomorrow.

Then I felt guilty about the worry and inconvenience my lie had caused. But as I lay miserably in the dark after the lights went out at 8:15 the idea came to me that all might not yet be lost. Throughout Tuesday hope waxed and waned repeatedly as nurses came and went, checking and recording my perfectly normal temperature and pulse.

That night Mum and Dad walked into the ward on the stroke of 7 o'clock. Dad looked pretty normal, but Mum could not conceal her worry with an exaggerated smile. She put her arms around me and hugged me fiercely. You'd think she knew I was going to die by the length and strength of that hug. I assured her I was not - that in fact I felt well enough to go home. That of course was true, as was my feeling of guilt at having involved my parents.

We made family conversation for a while, and they wanted to know all about the Charleville races and what Mr Henness and I had done. Dad was an amateur jockey, and he knew most of the racing men in Charleville and the other towns around the area. To Mum they were just names, but she was interested to know all about my recent adventure. She remarked how lucky it was that I didn't get sick while I was away in Charleville. It made me feel that I was lying again - to my mother - even though she was the one talking.

After a while, Dad drifted off to the adult end of the ward to talk to a patient called Gummy O'Brien. Gummy had a broken leg. He was a stockman and he had been thrown by a horse he was breaking in on Hoganthella Station. He and Dad had something in common because Dad had suffered a badly smashed collar bone while breaking in horses for thirty bob a week in the Depression – that was how he met Mum. He had to go to Brisbane for specialist treatment and Mum was working as a waitress in the kiosk at the Botanic Gardens. I didn't know what a kiosk was, but the way Mum talked about her job I knew it was much more stylish than Nick's Greek Café in Mitchell.

Anyway, as soon as Dad was out of earshot, I grabbed Mum's hand and blurted out my pleading confession: 'Mum, you've got to get me out of here! I'm not sick. I didn't have a pain in the stomach.'

She looked puzzled for a moment, but then she said,

'Merv, I know you are frightened of having the operation, but you needn't be. It won't hurt a bit. You won't feel a thing - in fact, you'll sleep right through it.'

'Mum,' I persisted with even more urgency, 'you don't understand. I shouldn't be in hospital. I told a lie.'

She grabbed my other hand and squeezed it. Then, as if she were talking about me to someone else, possibly gruff old Sergeant Bergen, investigating a petty theft or a broken window in our street, she said, 'If there's one thing I know about my boy – it is that he doesn't tell lies.'

'Mum,' I said desperately and slightly ashamed for her disappointment, 'I've just started lately.'

But Mum was having none of it.

She even argued that it was best to have my appendix out now than to have them burst in the Christmas holidays when I would be out mustering cattle with Dad on Winneba Station. If that happened, she added I could die of some sort of "itis" before they could get me to the hospital.

I promised they wouldn't burst, but it was no use and anyway, Dad was on his way back, so I had to give up arguing.

When they walked out the door when the lights were flicked off and on to signal the end of the visiting hour, I felt utterly abandoned. I knew that my self-inflicted fate, dreadful as it was to contemplate, had been sealed.

I have to admit that when the lights went out at 9 o'clock I pulled the blankets over my head and had a bit of a cry.

The main thing that happened on Wednesday was starvation. Nurse Waldron, who had been one of the big girls at St Patrick's Convent when I started school brought me a slice of toast and a cup of weak tea for breakfast.

'After this you will only have water until after the operation,' she announced rather cheerfully. 'You need to have an empty stomach for an appendix operation.'

I supposed they wouldn't want mushy half-digested

food spilling everywhere when the doctor cut your stomach open. The thought made me clutch my stomach with both hands. I still didn't know which side of me was going to be sliced open.

On Thursday morning at half-past seven, the beautiful Sister Gillespie came to my bedside and said she was going to prepare me for surgery.

She drew back the bedclothes and gently pulled down my pyjama pants, thankfully to just above my groin, and began to shave a rectangle on my right-side solar plexus. I knew the term from listening to the Friday night fights at the Brisbane Stadium on our little His Master's Voice mantel radio. Boxers attacked the solar plexus to wind their opponents and cause them to drop their hands, which left them open to a left hook or a right cross. Elly Bennet, the aboriginal Australian champion, specialised in that punch.

Of course, I was not thinking about all that boxing knowledge while Sister Gillespie was shaving my solar plexus. She probably wouldn't have been interested in it, anyway.

The shaving took only a couple of minutes. I don't think there was any hair on my stomach, so it was probably just something they always did to satisfy the doctor.

Finally, as she painted the shaved area with iodine, the most beautiful woman in Mitchell - I knew for sure now that Mum had been right about that - announced that she was starting her holidays when she came off duty in the afternoon and would not be seeing me again.

I felt such a pang of disappointment that I wondered if my survival instinct had been seriously weakened. Like most of the men in Mitchell, I was in love with Sister Gillespie.

About half an hour later in huffed Nurse Daly and, behind her, Nurse Waldron pushing a stretcher on wheels. I thought the stretcher was unnecessary because I had been thinking, even after the painting of my stomach, that it might not be too late to make a break for the bush, which came tantalisingly close to the hospital on three sides.

But when I stood up beside the bed, my legs felt shaky. The nurses hoisted me onto the stretcher and Nurse Daly told me to relax. I thought that even a tough bushranger like Ned Kelly would not be able to relax in this situation.

The trundle journey around the verandah to the operating theatre was disappointingly short. Nurse Daly pressed the button beside the door, and it opened to reveal Dr Williams and Matron Frawley in their starched white aprons and with their masks hanging around their necks. They looked so neat and spotless that I realised I was the first victim of the morning. My mouth felt very dry.

The nurses lifted me off my high trundle bed on to the operating table which was the same height. I thought at once it was not built for sleeping on - it was too hard by far - almost like lying on the floor.

Dr Williams didn't greet me by name, even though he could see my name on my wristband. And he was the first one to see me when I was born. But he probably wouldn't have recognised me because I had changed so much, and he'd probably seen a couple of hundred brand new babies since then.

The first thing he said was, 'Can you count boy?' I was quite taken aback. No-one had mentioned a maths test.

'I'm in Grade 5,' I said, thinking he'd taken me for a pre-schooler, or one of those lucky kids who lived on stations far from town and didn't go to school at all.

He must have thought I was being cheeky because he came back with a gruff, 'I didn't ask you that. I said, can you count?'

I knew he had the upper hand, and I certainly didn't want to upset him, but I did think momentarily that he should know that you don't get to Grade 5 without being able to count. So, I just replied meekly, 'Yes, I can count

Doctor.' I put the word "doctor" in because I didn't want him to be mad at me when he did the operation.

He sprinkled some drops from a small brown bottle on to a white pad that looked like Mum's powder puff and said, 'Let's see if you can count to sixty while I hold this over your nose and mouth. Breathe normally.

I didn't think I had breathed normally since Monday morning, and I was pretty sure that holding a wad of something over my nose and mouth would not make it any easier. But I resolved to reach sixty in record time just to show him why I was the second smartest kid in our class. Margaret Schneider, the chemist's daughter, always came top.

I set off briskly for 1, 2 and 3, but 4 was noticeably slow to pronounce and 5 even slower. I don't think I got to the "ks" sound of 6.

Nurse Waldon told me next day it was the chloroform on the powder puff that put me to sleep. She said some kids didn't get to four, so that was a bit of a consolation.

After the counting, the next thing I knew was being back in my bed vomiting clear liquid - there was obviously nothing else in my stomach - into a shiny kidney tray held under my chin by Nurse Waldron.

Although I would have much preferred the attentions of Sister Gillespie, she was kind and sympathetic. She gave me a damp, white hospital face-washer to wipe my face and said, 'You'll be nauseous for a while, but you'll be fine in the morning. Everything went well.'

I couldn't help asking, 'Was my appendix really bad?' I think I was hoping for some sort of personal redemption, some private, accidental justification for the lie. That perhaps, without showing any symptoms, my appendix had been about to burst the way Mum had said they could, and that perhaps by some sixth sense, I had lied just in the nick of time.

But it was not to be. Nurse Waldron replied, 'No, your appendix looked perfectly healthy. It was nice and plump and there was no sign of inflammation. It is in methylated spirits in a bottle in the operating theatre. I'll take you round on Sunday, and you can see for yourself if you like.'

I said I would like that and on Sunday morning she wheeled me round to the thankfully deserted operating theatre and pointed to my appendix sitting innocently in the metho. It looked exactly like the witchetty grubs we sometimes found when Dad split a log while getting firewood from over the river.

I asked Nurse Waldron if my appendix would grow again. She shook her head and said, with a convincing air of finality, 'No, it's gone for good now. But you didn't need it. It didn't do anything, so you won't miss it.'

It felt a bit weird seeing a part of myself there in the bottle - certainly more disconcerting than putting a tooth in a glass of water beside the bed for the tooth fairy. There was no comparison really. Firstly, the tooth had invariably come loose or been accidentally knocked out. My appendix, though apparently useless, was there because I had lied. It could have stayed inside me forever.

With a tooth, apart from the satisfying expectation of a financial reward, there was the reassurance of a new one pushing up to replace it. My appendix, as Nurse Waldron had said, was gone for good.

I consoled myself by thinking it was lucky that I hadn't expanded the lie about being sick to include a sore throat. At least I had kept my tonsils by sheer good fortune. It occurred to me that, once you start lying about yourself, you can easily do a lot of unintended damage.

Back in the end bed in the ward that afternoon I thought about some of the things Nurse Waldron had said. It struck me as being a bit odd that God must have made Adam with something that he didn't need in his solar plexus - especially something prone to exploding and causing kids to die young.

But then I remembered that God got pretty tired when he was making everything, and our catechism said that "on the sixth day he rested". So, I thought that he might have just forgotten to take out the unnecessary part before he went to sleep.

Anyway, although he wasn't a Catholic, old Dr Williams was doing a thorough job of fixing up God's mistake in Mitchell kids. Not just the sick ones, but healthy liars as well.

MATES

The Whites, Mr Jim White and his wife Sis, were our next-door neighbours. That was an approximation to which we attached no significance. They would have really been our next-door neighbours if their cottage had faced Ann Street as our house did, and if there hadn't been that spare allotment between our house and theirs. As it was, the back of their house faced the side of ours, but as there was only open space between, we thought of the Whites as our next-door neighbours.

Not that we were ever close to the Whites in the way we were friends with our other neighbours, Hec and Lily Carlyon who lived in the high house behind ours on Alice Street, or Lil and Harry Wilson and their boys who rented from the Carlyons at one stage. I remember we went over to comfort Lil - well Mum did the comforting - when her baby boy Leslie - named after the then Governor of Queensland, Sir Leslie Wilson - died. He was only three weeks old. He was laid out in the christening gown he never got to wear for his christening, in a little white coffin on the dining room table. The coffin was trimmed with curves and swirls painted in gold. But no one seemed to be much comforted by that. Little Leslie was a bluish-yellow colour. Mum said that was because he died of yellow jaundice.

Anyway, the Whites weren't there. They may not have even known that little Leslie Wilson had died after being in our neighbourhood for just a couple of weeks. I'm sure they would have heard about it eventually, and no doubt, they would have felt sorry for the Wilsons. I think they were kind enough people. We just weren't close to them. For instance, we never borrowed anything - a cup of sugar or a wedge of butter - as we sometimes did from Hec and Lily, Harry and Lil or Mrs Mauritz who was really our next-door neighbour on the other side. Of course, we always paid back the butter or whatever, and we always reciprocated whenever they needed to borrow some essential item from us. And, from time to time, as neighbours we shared our surpluses - home-grown vegetables, eggs, preserved fruit, or home-made jam or pickles.

I think Mum once sent me to the Whites' with a billy of soup when she knew, somehow, that Mrs White was not well. Other than on that occasion, I don't remember ever being in their house yard.

But in my boyhood, Mr Jim White was what could definitely be called a "significant other".

He was a short, thick-set man in his sixties. He had a mop of coarse unruly grey hair, a squarish face to match his body, and a short beard with a brownish-yellow nicotine stain which spread from where he held his cigarette holder clenched between his teeth in the corner of his mouth to the very tip of that grey stubble.

Jim White was, or had been, a shearer. Now he worked in the shearing sheds around Mitchell, variously as a shedhand, a roustabout or a picker-up. There were at least two shearing contractors in Mitchell in the forties and fifties. One was Marcus McManus, and the other, I think, was Austin Brennan. They both had large teams of shearers. I'm not sure which contractor had Jim White on his team – but he was out of town working in the sheds most of the year. Sometimes his wife, Sis, would also be out in a shed cooking for the shearers. Like Australia back then, the Whites "rode on the sheep's back".

When they were home, we saw little of Mrs White. In fact, when we did see her hanging out the washing or pottering about the yard there was very little of her to see. She was tiny and she kept to herself. Mum used to say, 'She wouldn't harm a mouse.' I took it to mean that she was a kind and gentle soul. She probably was too, but none of us, not even Mum, got to really know her.

I had a bit more to do with Mr White because, though our paths didn't actually cross, they often ran parallel. I suppose it was because I spent a fair bit of time outside the house, running the messages on my bike, bringing the cow home from The Common, or riding my pony around the neighbourhood. And, when he was in town, Jim White went down town most days and spent a fair bit of time in the pubs. Not that I spent much time in the pubs myself at ten or eleven, but I would see him on the way home late in the afternoon making his erratic way along Ann Street.

He always dressed up in a brown, pin-striped, double-breasted suit and wore a white shirt and a tie. The suit was a bit too big for him and the cuffs of his trousers were worn to threads at the back from being walked on. Even in the mornings when he headed off to town all spruced up, he looked a bit thrown together.

But in the afternoon on his way home he usually looked a wreck! His tie would be pulled halfway down his chest, his shirt unbuttoned, and his shirttails would be hanging out all around. Often, he would be clutching the day's shopping under both arms as he staggered this way and that in the middle of the road. Watching him you got the impression that the parcels under his arms were having a tug-of-war, pulling him first one way then the other.

And all the time he would be muttering to himself. Now and again, he would curse loudly at some invisible antagonist. At those times he was a frightening spectacle to us kids.

I remember asking Mum what would happen when he got home. Would he hurt Mrs White? Mum said, 'Don't worry love. He'll fall straight onto his bed and go to sleep as he is. Mrs White will take his shoes off and he will sleep like a baby all night in his good clothes.' I wondered if he would be surprised in the morning to wake up and find himself already dressed for town.

One afternoon though, I remember well. It was wintertime and the days were getting shorter, so the sun had almost gone when old Jim came staggering homewards. He had a parcel of meat under his arm, but he must have dropped it once or twice because a string of sausages had escaped and the last two or three were being dragged along the ground behind him.

Mum hurried out to tell him and offer him a brown paper bag to put the sausages in. He stopped, cocked his head on one side, apparently to bring Mum into focus, and said, 'Scuse the French Mishus Wesh. But you can't even trust bloody newspaper these days.' Anyway, Mum put the sausages into the bag and Jim gallantly doffed his hat in appreciation before he set off on the short stagger home - and, probably, bed.

Often, after that, if something were dropped or spilled accidentally at our place, someone would say, 'You can't even trust bloody newspaper these days.' And of course, we would all have a laugh.

Another time, I was schooling Elsie Carlyon's chestnut pony - Jiminy Cricket - in preparation for the "Pony Hunt" at the upcoming Mitchell Show. My mate Kenny Barber and I had built a practice jump in the spare allotment between our place and the Whites'.

It was fairly early in the afternoon so I am not sure why Jim would be coming home at that hour. But he was and, of course, he stopped to watch me put the pony over the hurdle. Actually, we had just raised the top rail as Jiminy

Cricket was clearing the previous height with ease. This time though, he baulked - skidding to a halt at the moment before take-off. I took him back to have another run at it, slapping him down the shoulder with a switch off the peach tree for encouragement. But he baulked again. By this time Mr White had climbed through the fence and was insisting that he put the pony over the jump.

Kenny and I tried our best to dissuade him. The saddle, as well as the pony, was too small we argued. We didn't mention what we both knew - that he was too drunk.

Anyway, next thing he scrambled aboard Jiminy Cricket, insisted I give him the peach switch as a persuader, and turned the pony to the run up. He came up the approach, arms flapping, coat tails flying behind him and flailing the air with the switch. At the very last moment the pony did exactly what it had done before - shot both front legs out stiffly and planted them stubbornly in front of the hurdle. But the hapless rider, far too well-dressed for the occasion, flew over the pony's head and landed in the dust on the other side of the hurdle. Mr White had cleared the hurdle easily and landed with a grunt, flat on his belly.

For a moment Kenny and I were terrified, thinking we might have let him be killed before our eyes. But in a surprisingly short time he rolled over, stood unsteadily upright, and began dusting off his double-breaster. Before walking crookedly off in disgust, he pronounced emphatically, 'That bloody horse will never make a jumper.'

Strangely though, to my great delight, Jiminy Cricket and I won the Pony Hunt Under 14 Hands at the Mitchell Show a few weeks later. I don't know if Mr White was there to see it.

As time went by, Jim White and I developed a "distant friends" kind of relationship, mainly because of my riding. When I was about eleven years old Dad was training a very good race mare called Lady Eagle. Fortunately, the black mare was very quiet and tractable, so I was able to ride her at exercise. Often Dad would be away from home for a period, and I would be in complete charge of the horse.

I used to give her long trotting in the sandy lane out past the cemetery. To get there I would ride out past the Whites' cottage in the early morning. Often old Jim would be out on their tiny verandah, not much more than a porch really, with a smoke in his cigarette holder and steam rising off a mug of tea. His greeting was always the same. 'Here comes Todd Sloane. G'Day Todd.'

I had never heard of Todd Sloane. But I assumed he was a jockey, because I was riding past the Whites' place on a sleek black racehorse. Years later I discovered the worth of the complimentary comparison. Todd Sloane was widely regarded as the best jockey in the world in the early decades of the 20th century.

An American, he reached the pinnacle of his trade in his home country and later rode with great success in England. Todd Sloane was the first jockey to adopt the "monkey crouch", riding with short stirrup leathers high over the horse's withers. It is the style used universally by jockeys to this day.

Of course, if I had known all that at the time Mum would have had to buy me a new school hat at Short and Hobson's General Store. I certainly would have had a "swelled head'.

Sometimes old Jim would add 'You'll win the Melbourne Cup one day son.' It gave me a thrill to think of it and I began to feel grateful for his admiration. In fact, I was disappointed on the mornings when he was missing from the verandah - either out in the sheds or still asleep in his going-out clothes.

I distinctly remember having a dream about that time. In my dream I was going to ride in the Melbourne Cup, and I had promised Mum I would buy her a refrigerator if I won. Well, in the dream I rode the winner of the Cup. Trotting back to scale and the deafening applause of the crowd at Flemington - it's a wonder it didn't wake me up! I was thinking how proud Mum would be back in Mitchell, listening to the race on our little His Master's Voice mantel radio.

To my delighted surprise, as I approached the gate to the saddling enclosure, I spied Jim White in his brown, pin-striped, double-breaster sitting on the fence waving his bowler hat in jubilation. As I rode past, he shouted 'Good on you Todd. I knew you'd do it mate.' I felt momentarily embarrassed for both of us. I knew he shouldn't be sitting on the saddling paddock fence at Flemington. You couldn't even do that at the Mitchell races.

But the brief feeling of unease was quickly displaced by a surge of gratitude for his loyalty and pride in the fact that I had fulfilled his oft-repeated prophesy, 'You'll win the Melbourne Cup one day son.'

In that moment I knew that Jim White and I had become mates.

MEMORABLE MITCHELL CHARACTERS

Step 'N Fetchit

Did anyone else call her by that unkind name? Or was it just Dad and me, one time each?

Looking up from digging a garden bed for Mum, sweat running down his cheeks and dripping off his nose he said, as if announcing it to the summer heat, 'There she goes, old "Step 'n Fetchit.' And I looked out to the sandy lane that was our street, Ann Street, and saw her hurrying towards town along beside the fence on the far side.

She was dressed, as usual, in a grey cotton dress. It may have been the only one she owned. The dress had long sleeves and fell almost to her ankles. But the skirt was pretty full, and it in no way impeded her speedy progress. Her grey hair was bunched up at the back in a loose bun and she wore her usual floppy navy rag hat. The hat hid most of her profile, so it could almost have been a dress and hat getting along on their own.

But they were going too fast to be doing it by themselves, and there was no wind. Step 'n Fetchit leaned forward as she hurried along, always seeming to be looking for something on the ground a few paces ahead of her. Her sandshoes occasionally scuffed up a little cloud of dust in front of her.

When I was little, I wondered why she hurried. One day I tried to slow her down, to get her to look up or perhaps say hello or wave.

From my red pedal car on our front verandah, I called out, 'G'Day Step 'n Fetchit' and when she took no notice, I called out again, more loudly, 'G'Day Step 'n Fetchit'. She either didn't hear me, or she chose to ignore my bold greeting, because she just kept going towards whatever it was on the ground ahead and the shops. She didn't even look up. 'Perhaps she's deaf,' I thought.

But in the next moment I found out that Mum wasn't deaf. It was one of the few times that she punished me. Hurrying from the kitchen, her hair and face damp with perspiration, she made me get out of the car, gave me a hard smack on the bottom, and made me sit in the washhouse. As she followed me to that lonely penitentiary, she asked me where I had heard the name that I had used in my shouted, wasted greeting.

When I told her she said, 'Your father should know better. Don't ever call the poor woman by that name again. It is not her name and it's unkind to say it.'

I never called her Step 'n Fetchit again, and I think Mum must have given Dad a good talking-to, because I never heard him say it again, either.

Sometime later, I learned that her name was Ethel Symes. She was a spinster who lived alone in a faded pink weatherboard cottage on the riverbank out past the cemetery.

When I was old enough to wander more freely with my schoolmates, we would spend a lot of our free time along the river. It didn't matter that it was usually just a broad, sandy bed of noogoora burr between the banks. It had an aura of adventure that drew us – there were birds' nests high in the trees and we built forts and made primitive wooden sledges to slide down the steep shaley banks.

Sometimes we would see Ethel Symes outside in her small backyard. She kept some chooks, and she had a brown kelpie watchdog. Otherwise, she was totally alone in that isolated place. She would be in the yard until she saw us and then she would hurry inside. Some of the bigger boys said she had a rifle, and when she saw anyone coming, she would go inside and load it. We never gave her cause to shoot.

When I was older, I sometimes worried about her. Who were her parents? Did she ever have a family like ours - brothers and sisters I mean? And if she did, what happened? Why was she so completely alone? Who would know if she got sick, or even worse, died? Did anyone ever love her?

We moved further west to Mungallala when I was thirteen, and the following year I went away to boarding school. I forgot about Ethel Symes. Now I wonder what happened to her.

I thought of her again in 2012 - when Mitchell was inundated by a massive flood. The river broke its banks out past the racecourse and swept through the town, inundating three-quarters of the houses to the roof-tops.

Ethel Symes would have been long gone, but I could imagine her old pink cottage being swept along, rocking and swaying on the raging muddy waters of the mighty Maranoa, only to smash and break apart against the red railway bridge when it reached the town.

I was pleased to think she'd hurried away from that calamity - for, if she hadn't drowned, it would have broken her heart.

Bill Doonan

Bill Doonan was another "river dweller" when I was a youngster in Mitchell. He was a middle-aged bachelor who had what adults referred to as a "settler's block" on the other side of the river and a few miles to the west of Ethel Symes' pink cottage. His home was more like a hut than a house and, from a distance, looked as if it might have grown out of the ground. It had a dusty tumble-down look about it.

The most remarkable thing about Bill Doonan was his eyes. He was an average sort of man when you saw him from a distance or from the side. I mean by his height and his weight.

But front on and close up you could see those unblinking sky-blue eyes, so flat and dull they could have been made of the plasticine we were sometimes allowed to play with at school. Bill Doonan was blind. Mum said it was an accident with acid that left the poor fellow sightless.

He would ride past our place – up against the fence on the other side of our sandy lane, Ann Street – tapping on the top wire with a switch from a sapling. That was how he found his way once he got on the town side of the river. Where there was no fence to guide him, he must have relied on his memory for direction and distance. Dad said he knew his settler's block like the 'back of his hand'. I wondered how that could be since he couldn't even see his hands.

Bill Doonan always rode a young thoroughbred - not the same one, though the horses always looked similar. They were always coal black or such a dark brown that they could pass for black, always gangly, lightly framed and skittish. Mum was always afraid that Mr Doonan would get thrown and be injured. But it never happened.

Dad said that Bill Doonan was a pretty good horseman, but he broke his horses in too young. Instead of letting them grow until they were at least two or three years old, he would break them in at eighteen months. Dad said that was like sending kids to school at three and expecting them to learn to read and write. Not that Dad was an expert on learning at school. He was only ten when he left school and went droving. But that was why Bill Doonan's horses were so skittish. Everything around them was new - especially when he rode them into town the first few times - and that was why they shied and sometimes ran backwards in fright. It was when they reared up in protest at something unfamiliar in front of them that I got the biggest fright. But Bill Doonan would just lean forward as they reared up, and when their front feet hit the ground again, he would slap them on the rump with the switch and drive them forward. Sometimes there would be a battle of wills for ten minutes or so, but Bill Doonan always won. I suppose he had to because he had to get supplies from the shops. I don't think I ever saw his mount bail up on the way home. No doubt they knew they were going towards the freedom of the horse paddock and perhaps even a dipper of oats.

My old brown pony Gertie was like that anyway. I needed a pepperina switch to get her to go properly on the way to the shops. But on the way home I just had to hold on and hope that the groceries, especially the eggs, would be intact when her rough gallop ended at the water trough on The Common near our place. I think she was addicted to lucerne hay and molasses - a portion of which I gave her every evening during the cold Mitchell winters.

One time I recall Bill Doonan having one of his light-framed thoroughbreds at the races. I don't remember its name or where it finished in its race - if indeed it started. But it was very nervous. It was trembling and pawing the sand with its front feet as it stood in the bower-shed tie-up stalls. It dug a hole so deep that it looked like a Shetland pony at its withers. Other horses did the same thing, but I had never seen one dig a hole as big as Bill Doonan's horse did that day.

When our family left Mitchell in 1950 and moved the twenty-eight miles further west to Mungallala Bill Doonan was still going strong, riding past on the far side of the road, tapping on the fence with his sapling switch. After we moved, I boarded with our neighbours the Colvilles - a dear and gentle older couple. They lived right at the end of our street. Not in it but facing it. Was their street called Rugby Street? Anyway, I still saw Bill Doonan riding past occasionally on a Saturday morning.

At the end of the year, I went home to my family in Mungallala for the school holidays. Then it was off to boarding school in Toowoomba for the next four years.

I had almost no contact with Mitchell during those school years and, even though I taught in Mitchell for four or five months in my first year of teaching, I never really took up where I'd left off as a carefree thirteen-year-old whose only ambition had been to be a jockey.

Bill Doonan was part of my losses from those happy and occasionally scary times. I wonder what happened to him. Did he just grow old and die alone or was it something more newsworthy like being thrown or smashed into a tree by a skittish thoroughbred too young to be broken in, but strong enough to kill a man in fright - a blind man anyway?

Pirie Pickup

Pirie Pickup? Was that his real name? I wonder now if it might have been some Mitchell wag's substitution for something much more elegant. Perhaps Pierre Picoult? Pirie Pickup could have been a French scientist like Louis Pasteur, stranded in Mitchell by an addiction to rum compounded by an affliction called St Vitus Dance.

Anyway, Pirie Pickup was the most frightening figure in my small Mitchell world when I was in the lower grades at school.

He was over six feet tall and thin as a string. He wore a grey felt hat with a wide, black band and a floppy, moth-eaten brim. He usually wore a greyish-white, long-sleeved shirt, the tail of which often hung out and flapped frantically behind him.

His brown or black striped serge trousers, held above his bony hips by what could have been the cord out of his pyjama pants, flapped about his ankles in what appeared to be a determined attempt to trip him up.

On his sockless feet he wore sandshoes that allowed several toes of each foot to see daylight. They, the shoes, always looked in need of a touch of Meltonian Shoe Cream which we kids used to apply to our own Dunlop sandshoes in preparation for tennis or cricket at school.

Pirie Pickup lived in a tiny house - not much more than a humpy really - in our sandy lane called Ann Street. His thousand-gallon water tank, streaked with rust, was almost as big as the house itself. Sometimes I wondered if he could lie down inside to sleep at night. But I supposed he must have.

Pirie Pickup didn't mean to frighten us kids. He just couldn't help it. I wonder if he knew just what terror he struck into us. I doubt it. Most of the time he seemed oblivious of his surroundings - lost in a strange world of his own.

Some of the big kids called him "the Meccano man". In those days, many boys had Meccano sets. Meccano was the predecessor to the modern, universally popular construction toy, Lego. A Meccano set consisted of a large assortment of light metal plates or bars of varying lengths and usually painted green, lined with holes to take the tiny bolts and nuts necessary to hold them in place in the construction of tractors, cranes, bridges and the many ambitious building projects that young boys undertook on their bedroom floors.

Actually, while the term "Meccano man" was somewhat disrespectful, it was also remarkably apt. Even when he was standing "still" Pirie Pickup was all points and angles. And when he was walking, often staggering, he was a dramatic display of moving parts - legs jerking erratically and arms flailing in what appeared to us kids to be a one-man assault on the universe.

And, as he walked, or jerked along, rarely in a straight line, he made a clicking noise with his voice that suggested there was a motor somewhere inside him, or, if he were a real Meccano man, some screws needed tightening.

Of course, you couldn't hear the "motor" when he was muttering to himself, shouting at his invisible enemies or, as we usually imagined, ourselves.

One day I remember quite vividly. It was a hot Mitchell afternoon and my sister Maureen and I were trudging home from school. We had just passed Granny Munro's high house with the palm trees in the front yard. We were heading to the corner where Mr Pascoe, the bootmaker, lived, to turn into our street when we both saw, at the same time, Pirie Pickup lying flat out in the hot sun. He was just outside the Pascoe's front fence. And for once, he wasn't moving.

Maureen was all for leaving him alone and telling Mum when we got home. But I said, 'He might be dead.' I was thinking it would be good to be able to tell my mate Spank Rush and the others at school that I had found a dead man. And, probably taking courage from the thought, I started to walk slowly towards his prostrate form.

'Come back Merv!' Maureen hissed. 'He might grab you.' That slowed me down a bit. But "screwing my courage to the sticking point", to borrow a phrase from Shakespeare's Lady Macbeth - she would have been proud of me - I tiptoed towards the sound asleep, possibly even dead, Pirie Pickup.

I'm not sure what I was going to do. I certainly wasn't going to touch him or tug his shirtsleeve to wake him up. I think I was going to have a fairly close look - just to see if his chest was moving to show he was breathing. If he had been breathing, I wouldn't have disturbed him, even though he must have been very hot lying out there in the summer sun. Looking back, it was clearly more curiosity than charity that motivated my risky behaviour.

Anyway, I was probably only a few feet away from him - I could smell the sharp rum fumes - when he suddenly sprang into loud and spectacular action. Both arms shot straight up in the air, his legs buckled up and he arched his back and began to bounce up and down and shout abuse as if it were not just me, but the whole town that enraged him at that moment.

He probably didn't even see me because that was the day Maureen and I set the unofficial, unbeatable record for the three-quarter-mile dash by siblings under seven from Pascoe's corner to No.2 Ann Street. Maureen kept pace with me, and we didn't stop 'til we reached our own front gate. 'I told you you shouldn't,' she said, catching her breath as we hurried onto our front verandah.

She couldn't wait to tell Mum, blurting it out as soon as we got inside. 'Pirie Pickup nearly grabbed Merv,' she said, wide-eyed and still puffing from the frantic run. 'Pirie Pickup was lying down near Mr Pascoe's fence and Merv went over to see if he was dead. I told him not to. Pirie Pickup woke up and I think he was really mad at Merv because he started yelling at him and waving his arms and kicking.'

Mum just told us to take off our school bags and go and wash our red faces.

When we got back to the kitchen there were two glasses of orange cordial on the table and four jam drops - two each of our favourites.

As we ate and drank Mum told us what she thought had happened. She said 'Poor Mr Pickup probably had too much to drink. Sometimes when men have too much to drink, they have to sleep it off. Mr Pickup just didn't get home in time to do it. Anyway, he wasn't angry with you Merv. He may have the "DTs".'

'What's that?' we chorused at once.

'It's like bad dreams,' Mum said. 'When men have too much to drink, they often imagine that bad things are happening. Poor Mr Pickup was probably dreaming of demons and goodness knows what other terrible things just when Merv got close to him. He probably didn't even know Merv was there.'

I was relieved to hear that last bit because I was already wondering if I'd made a permanent enemy of Pirie Pickup and hoping I hadn't. After all, we used to pass each other fairly regularly on my way to and from school, and sometimes when I had to go to the shops to do the messages for Mum. The lane always seemed too narrow at those times.

Nothing like that ever happened again. I never actually saw Pirie Pickup lying down beside the road again. That must have been the only time he didn't make it home in time to have the "DTs".

What happened to him, I wonder? Like 'Step 'n Fetchit' - the hurrying Ethel Symes, and the blind horseman - Bill Doonan, Pirie Pickup was a solitary figure. Something of a hermit really, jittering along in the memories of my Mitchell boyhood, like a Meccano man.

Walter

It was a stinking hot day when they buried Walter. There wasn't a breath of air in the little, cream, red-roofed, weatherboard St John's Church of England.

Walter probably hadn't been there since Frances, the last of his three nieces – the Cullen sisters – had walked down the aisle to marry Alby Duncan.

Walter wasn't a churchgoer. He may not have even been christened.

That didn't seem to bother the Minister, who made a pretty good fist of confirming the worthiness of a man about whom he knew nothing.

The church wasn't full. Only two or three front pews were occupied. The Cullens were there. Herb and Lois and of course the nieces and their husbands. There were probably half a dozen mourners outside the family.

Walter wasn't exactly a recluse, but he didn't have many friends - only the neighbours really. Perhaps it was his speech impediment, or maybe his obesity, which caused him to withdraw a little, keep to himself.

He was a bachelor of course and a neighbour. I remember him from my earliest years. He lived alone in a house at the end of Alice Street - adjacent to the cemetery. He would go past his whole life on the way to his grave on this blistering afternoon.

Sometimes he worked as a shearers' cook in the sheds around Mitchell. That was the only work he did. The Minister didn't mention this.

When I was a small boy, before I started school, Walter used to often do some shopping for Mum. He was quite a regular shopper and Mum hardly ever went downtown. There was always plenty to do at home with us kids - three or four under five - and Mum didn't have many good dresses. When I was about four Mum would give me a shopping list and Walter would take me with him.

That was about the time I noticed his habit of rubbing his hand up and down the front of his trousers. He would do it several times as he waddled along the sandy path beside the chook house to the little wooden gate of our house-yard.

One day after we got back from the shops and Walter had gone home, I asked Mum, 'Why does Walter rub his belly up and down on his way to our place?'

She said, 'Poor Walter is making sure he's decent before he gets here. He can't see whether all his fly buttons are done up, so he checks them with his fingers.'

We males all had button-up flies in our pants back then. I had one button in my good navy serge pants. With my play shorts I had to lift up one of the legs to pee. That was much more convenient, but it would not have been possible for Walter, who never wore shorts in his whole life. At least not after I was born. He always wore long trousers held up below his large belly by braces.

I remember thinking I hope I never get as fat as Walter. It must be a worry not to be certain you are "decent", as Mum put it.

In the stifling heat, and the drone of the Minister's voice, the memories flooded back. How on Saturday mornings when we had finished our shopping, Walter would go to the Roses' Café for an ice-cream sundae. It was three scoops of vanilla ice-cream arranged to form a pyramid, surrounded by red and green jelly and topped with crushed nuts. My mouth would water as I sat on the step at the front door of the Café and watched Jean Rose carry the technicolour delight on a tray, perched on her conveniently protruding right hip, to Walter's table. He would sit facing the door - and me - as he savoured every spoonful, and scraped the bottom of the elegant, boat-shaped serving dish for every last, delicious drop.

He always smiled a satisfied smile when Jean came, tray on that shelf-like hip, to take the serving dish and the long-handled teaspoon - we didn't have any of those in our cutlery drawer at home.

Poor Jean Rose. She was a tall, thin spinster with brown hair and a serious face, more suited to a nun or a schoolteacher than a waitress. Her torso swung away from her right hip and only straightened sufficiently at the shoulders to let her hold her neck and head up straight.

Being just a little fellow, I thought that it was probably because she had carried so many trays on that hip; but it was really a physical deformity caused by a very difficult birthing - perhaps too sharp a tug on the forceps - or a crippling illness in childhood.

When Walter came out of the Café, he would always say something like 'Dat tundy was bootiful', or 'Oo can't beat a Tundy on a Tatdy'. I believed him and always wished I'd shared the experience.

One Saturday I prevailed upon him to let me come in and just sit at the table with him. He was reluctant to let me, but in the end gave in on the condition that I, 'Tit dere and tay nutting.'

When Jean came over and asked Walter what he would like - I thought she should remember because he had the same delicious treat every Saturday - he said, as he probably always did, 'A Tundy on a Tatdy pwease Dean.'

Then the lovely Jean Rose smiled at me and asked, 'What would you like young man?'

'I wish I could have a Tundy on a Tatdy, like Walter,' I said - not thinking she would take a wish as an order.

She said, 'I thought you might,' and turned away before Walter could get a shocked word out.

'I wir pobly have to pay for dat.' And, as it turned out, he did.

He said, 'Oo are a naughty boy. Oo said oo would tay nutting. I wir ter or mudder on oo.'

He kept saying it all the way home.

But all I could think of was the thrill of having that delicious treat put in front of me and the joy of every slow spoonful. I knew it would never happen again but even that thought couldn't spoil the happiness of that Saturday morning.

One other occasion, when Walter and I were "at odds" so to speak, occurred one night when he was minding us kids. Mum and Dad must have been out for some unusual reason. They almost never went out at night. Dad was rarely home anyway. He worked on stations as a stockman and would be away sometimes for months. And Mum was a busy, working-class mother who usually had chores to do at home in the evenings – like ironing, darning socks, or mending clothes. I have no idea what took them out this particular night, but Walter was our "baby-sitter", though I don't think that term had been invented back then. Anyway, he was looking after us kids - we weren't babies.

How old my sisters Maureen, Lola, Myril and I were, I'm not sure. I was apparently old enough to have, or make, a shanghai - a crude type of slingshot - but not old enough to handle it safely. We were sitting on the kitchen floor, and I had Walter bailed up with the shanghai – threatening his life with it I suppose. He was obviously frightened that I would let fly with the marble in the tongue of my catapult. He had his hands up to protect his face and was pleading, 'Put dat ding down Merdyn, I wir ter or mudda on oo.'

It was Maureen, younger than me by a year or so, who saved the situation. She shouted 'Don't shoot Merv. You'll knock your eye out!'

I had the shanghai pointing the wrong way and if I had let fly, I would have hit myself smack in the face.

Walter seized the moment and put me in a Half-Nelson, which was a crippling wrestling hold invented by the champion professional wrestler, Chief Little Wolf. He hooked my leg around the leg of the table and sat on my foot.

'Now oo da boss?' he taunted. 'Now oo da boss?'

The girls begged him to let me go but he would not be persuaded for a long time - and of course he had taken possession of the shanghai. I had a stiff leg for several days, but I wasn't game to complain about it.

That was the night we put a hole in the fibro cement - no doubt full of asbestos - with which Dad had very recently lined our kitchen walls. It was when Walter and I were wrestling, and of course Walter was quick to attach the blame to us kids. 'Now look wat oo done,' he said. 'Or farder wir be mad at oo.'

A few years later, when I was probably nine or ten, Dad had brought horses to Mitchell for the races. They were stabled at the back of Herb and Lois Cullen's where Walter was living at the time. I think Herb and Lois were working in the shearing sheds on stations around the district, and Walter was looking after the place. Anyway, one morning after we had worked the horses, hosed them off and fed them, we went upstairs to have some breakfast. Walter was sitting at the kitchen table with a roast leg of mutton, a loaf of bread and a pound of butter in front of him. Dad said, 'You must be on the tooth, Walter. That's a hearty breakfast you're having.'

Walter replied, without a hint of embarrassment, 'Deeda Tight Punt, a man dotta eat.'

Dad's name was Henry, but I probably didn't know it then. Everyone, even Mum, called him 'Punch". Walter couldn't quite finish it properly - to him Dad's name was always Punt. And the good man they crucified long ago was "Deeda Tight".

I don't know if the therapy available in schools today could have improved Walter's speech, but it would not have mattered anyway because Walter had never gone to school. He couldn't read or write. But he must have learned to count. People said he was very well off, but he was "tight." That meant he didn't throw his money around. And was probably why he was so furious about my treachery at the Roses' Café.

One interesting aspect of Walter's life escaped mention by the pale young Minister who conducted the burial service. To be fair, he probably had no inkling of it, and I doubt if anyone could have told him - except my mum. And she would not have told him anyway. Mum could be very close - especially when it came to guarding her friends from gossip. One of her maxims for us kids was 'You don't wash your dirty linen in public'. It didn't make much sense when I first heard her say it. Our two round, galvanised iron washtubs were on a bench in the washhouse at the back of our old brown house. Later, I came to understand it and I knew she meant, 'You don't wash other people's dirty linen in public either.' Mum had zero tolerance for gossip.

So, what dark secret had Walter kept from the world? You're probably not into gossip either, but you'll probably forgive my passing this on. And it is not going to trouble Walter now.

There was a period, I'm not sure how long it lasted, when Walter would come over to our place in the evening and sit on the lawn chatting with Mum. But his eyes and his attention were elsewhere. He always sat with his back to our kitchen so he could see the houses on the town side of our place in Ann Street. The house that he watched expectantly was a high, corrugated iron house that always looked to be in need of serious maintenance. Miraculously it was unscathed in the cyclone that unroofed half the buildings in Mitchell, including St Patrick's Convent School. The house, like many of that era, including our own at No. 2 Ann Street, consisted of two sections. The main part of the house, the dining room, if there were one, and the bedrooms were connected to the kitchen by a landing, or walkway, often, but not always, covered by a roof. Ours had a roof over it, but the house Walter was focussed on, had a narrow, rickety looking, uncovered "bridge" between the kitchen and the main house. The widow Sykes lived there with her large brood of children. She kept to herself, and the children were often a bit raggedy, but they were our playmates in the street after school and on weekends.

Eventually, if we had not been sent to bed, we would hear Walter say, 'Well Fweet,' (Mum's name was Freda) 'Ai be off now. Da cote i kear.' And, following his gaze, you could see a hurricane lantern being waved back and forth from that rickety Sykes' landing. When little Henry Sykes joined his excited siblings, he had an unusually large head and a profound speech impediment. I don't know if Walter took responsibility for his son, but I hope he had the decency to let the moths out of his wallet from time to time. The widow Sykes deserved at least that for allowing Walter the privilege of being a lover and a father.

My awareness of Walter's love life and paternity came much later than the events themselves. I was too young at the time to understand the significance of the waving lantern, except as a signal that Walter expected when the coast was clear. No doubt the kids had been safely stowed in their lumpy beds and the good widow Sykes was free to entertain her nightly visitor.

But the minister, and possibly all of the small group of mourners were unaware of Walter's romantic successes. I am not sure if it qualified as "dirty linen" or not, but I felt sure that Mum would have approved it being kept private.

I looked at the front row in time to see Herb Cullen's head droop forward and jerk up suddenly. He was obviously almost asleep. I thought to myself, 'It would probably stimulate some interest if the minister were suddenly to announce that in his middle age Walter had found a love of sorts and secretly fathered a son who was inarticulate.' But it was of course not to be - the announcement I mean.

And the ceremony over, we followed the coffin out to the hearse waiting in the blazing heat. Then we followed in just four cars - Mum would never let us count cars at a funeral - not even little David Lansdowne's who had been run down by an American jeep and must have been the record for vehicles at a Mitchell funeral. But with just the four cars you didn't have to count - you just knew.

At the cemetery it was like a reunion as we passed the headstones of people that we knew, and who would have known - or thought they knew - Walter. As they lowered the coffin into the sandy Mitchell ground, I thought, 'Walter had the last laugh. He was in the coolest place in town.'

Dave McAnelly

There were some characters who were part of the daily fabric of life in Mitchell when I was a boy. They were not particularly close to anyone, and they did not have any relatives around. Not like most of us who could claim aunts, uncles and cousins, if not in Mitchell, then in nearby towns like Amby, Mungallala and Morven.

Dave McAnelly was one such character. He did a fruit and vegetable run in a dray with a canvas hood like a

Romani (gypsy) wagon, pulled by a bay, half-draught horse.

Probably in his late fifties or early sixties, Dave had a gravelly voice and a drooping, light brown and grey moustache. He grew some of his produce himself on his orchard block on the edge of town. Some he got from "down below", the term used for the distant east, ending in Brisbane. Where did that expression come from? The land around Mitchell and all those western towns is dead flat as far as the eye can see. Was there an assumption that if you went far enough - to Brisbane anyway there would be a significant descent somewhere? I suppose there was really - the old toll-bar road down the range from Toowoomba. But no one ever explained the term "down below" in that way. The truth is I'm just now conjecturing about how it might have originated. When someone said, "down below" when I was a boy, I knew they meant "Brisbane" or somewhere "down there". I didn't think to ask, 'How far below?', or 'Below what?'

But back to Dave McAnelly and his fruit and vegie run. He rang a bell rather like our school bell to let the housewives know he was approaching. They would go out to the front gate where his old bay cart horse stopped by habit. The women would have a basket or hessian shopping bag for the produce they bought.

Mum would always try to buy a few things, especially local produce such as grapes, peaches, apricots and plums, when they were in season, as well as basic vegetables like potatoes, pumpkin and carrots or turnips. All of these we grew ourselves at times.

Dave always touched his hat and said, 'What'll it be today, Mrs Welch?' He would usually add something like 'The apples are from Stanthorpe - Granny Smiths, very sweet.' At first, I thought that some old grey-haired lady had grown them. The odd thing was it always sounded as if he were growling.

One time Dave McAnelly gave me a ride from "Warren

Point", a station owned by Mr Lethbridge. I think it was 12 or 15 miles south of Mitchell, so it was good to have the lift. Even so, my bottom was pretty sore by the time we got to town with the spring cart full of lettuce. The seat was a board supported by a bucket at each end, and the road was a winding bush track. Dave McAnelly must have had a tough backside!

He rattled on all the way. I suppose he was making the most of the opportunity to talk to someone other than his horse. Even though I was pretty young, he would have known I could understand English – which was more than his old bay horse could do.

The remarkable thing was that his voice, which sounded hoarse at the very start of the drive seemed to be just as strong when he croaked, 'Cheerio young man' as he set me down at our front gate.

I wonder what caused that voice problem. Did he have some serious deformity in the larynx from birth? Or when his voice "broke" at puberty did the breaking go on too long with the result that Dave's voice was not merely broken, but shattered for life?

Anyway, whenever I recall Dave McAnelly, I hear his throaty, river-gravel voice saying, 'What'll it be today, Mrs Welch? The apples from Stanthorpe, Granny Smiths, very sweet!'

I wonder what happened to him. Where did he end up? Is he resting in the sand at the river end of Alice Street with Walter and little Leslie Wilson? Perhaps I will go back one day and see if I can find him. Another cheerful ghost of my Mitchell boyhood.

Bernie Peeny

Bernie Peeny was the town carrier when I was a boy in Mitchell. He was a bachelor, and I can't even remember where he lived. But it wasn't on our side of the railway line. He must have lived somewhere down on the town side - somewhere between the main street, Cambridge Street, and the hospital where I had my appendix removed because I told a lie.

Bernie was a small man, a bit like an elf. He had a very small face and one short leg. I don't think it was a wooden leg - but he had a very peculiar walk. He seemed to rock to one side, wobble hesitantly, and then come back to a more or less vertical position. It was as if he were stepping over some obstacle every time he took a step with his short leg. Anyway, he must have been used to it because he was always busy, always on the move.

Like Dave McAnelly, Bernie Peeny had a horse and cart to do his carrying. When Dad bought our first car – a very second-hand 1928 Chev 4 Utility, he sold our blue dray to Bernie Peeny. It was the cart that we kids used to love riding in when Dad took us with him to cut firewood over the river. That always seemed to be an adventure - especially when Silver, our taffy half-draught mare, was pulling us up the steep banks of the Maranoa, or when she had to sit back into the britchen going down with a load of wood, sometimes a tub of honeycomb if Dad robbed a wild bees' hive, and us kids holding our seats and our breaths behind her.

Whenever I saw Bernie Peeny in our dray, I always felt a bit sad that our spring cart days were over. We did have some fun in the back of the Chev 4 which Dad painted green, but it was never quite as exciting as our rides in that old blue dray. I missed the smell of the mare as she broke out into a sweat from the exertion, and her snuffling and puffing when she was straining to pull us up the bank.

But Bernie Peeny was completely unaware of my disappointment that he now owned the dray. It probably wouldn't have bothered him anyway as he had no doubt paid Dad what he asked for it.

Bernie's main business was carrying goods from the railway to the grocery stores and cafes in Cambridge Street. For a little man, and partly a cripple, he must have been pretty strong. I can remember him man-handling bags of potatoes, onions and pumpkins destined for sale in Short and Hobson's and Hunters Pty Ltd, Mitchell's two main grocery stores.

But one of my favourite memories is of Bernie "walking" the green canvas drums of Peter's ice-cream, packed in something magical called "dry ice" across the footpath and up the step into the Roses' Café. He didn't lift and carry the puffy green cylinder. He stood it at an angle to himself and rolled it on the edge of its round base. He was smart that way!

Now that I think of it, Bernie Peeny brought all the good things down town from the Railway Station – the ice-cream, the ice-blocks, the lollies and chocolates, as well as all the less exciting essentials for our Mitchell households.

Was the carrying business his entire existence? I can't remember seeing him doing anything but carrying. I know he never went to the races. He just wasn't that sort of man. Though he was small enough to be a jockey. In England years ago he could have been a chimney sweep.

But I can't recall ever seeing him at the football on a Sunday or at the Show or at a circus. Did he have any social life? Did he go to church? He wasn't a Catholic, or if he was, he had lost the faith. I was an altar boy, and I knew all the people who attended Mass at Saint Columba's. Bernie wasn't among them.

In fact, despite his daily presence carrying in the main street, Bernie Peeny was a chronic social absentee.

Bernie wasn't there that night when it seemed the whole town was out on the plain near the town bore celebrating the end of World War II. They had a big bonfire going and were letting off crackers. It was much bigger than any Guy Fawkes Night because everyone was together, and it was like the town was putting on the fireworks.

Everyone seemed to be there. The Bank Manager, Mr

Sweeney, under his mop of frizzy black hair and still wearing his dove-grey business suit, white shirt and tie was in the thick of it. Even grumpy old Sergeant Bergen was joining in. He was still in uniform, but he wasn't wearing his hat - probably to show he wasn't really on duty, and he wasn't going to arrest anyone that night even if they got a bit too drunk. Even the reserved Miss Sims, Bill Mackay's tall, elegantly dressed Secretary - the gossip was that she was also his mistress - was laughing and hugging with everyone else.

It was a joyous occasion! Everyone was relieved and excited because the brave Mitchell soldiers, sailors and airmen who had escaped the Saturday morning Post Office Listings of those "Killed in Action" or "Missing in Action" would be coming home again.

And of course, we would soon be throwing away our ration coupon books.

It was a pity Bernie wasn't there that night because the grown-ups did a dance that was made for him. They lined up one behind the other holding on to the hips of the person in front. Then they moved forward in a jerky sort of jog kicking their free leg out to the side with every step. It looked as if they all had dislocated hips, as they jerked along singing "Don't Sit Under the Apple Tree" and "It's a Long Way to Tipperary". That was the first time I'd seen the dance called "The Conga". Bernie would have been good at it if he could have kept up with the others, but he wasn't there.

Now, as I look back, I wonder what happened to him. He would have died long ago no doubt. But did his life end in Mitchell or did he go away - "down below" - to live out his last years on the pension?

Did he ever have any friends? Family? Was he ever in love with someone? Did anybody ever love Bernie Peeny?

SATURDAYS – DAYS OF VIOLENCE

It started with the killing of the Rhode Island Red Rooster which had been Mum's pride until it attacked me - her precious baby boy - and almost pecked out my left eye.

I was probably close to two years old, but still wearing a nappy and sleeping in the black cot with the wooden slats and fixed sides. With some cots you could slide the side down to deposit or withdraw the infant. But ours was fixed solid - like the cogs on my Malvern Star fixed-wheel bike which I got six or seven years later when our boarder, the red-haired, freckle-faced Anthony Doonan got meningitis and ended up deaf. So, Mum had to lift me over the side of the cot. Not that it would have been a problem for her. Mum was a biggish woman - not fat, but big-boned and strong from hard work and long hours on her feet.

When Dad got home from Bonus Downs Station that Friday night, I was standing up in the cot holding onto the top rail. My head was swathed in a bandage, probably as big as the nappy I was wearing. Dad picked me up and held me to his bony chest and rubbed his whiskery face against my cheek. I guess it was supposed to feel good. It was the first thing I remember about being alive.

Next morning, I watched Dad as he knocked the Rhode Island Red on the head with the pot stick. That was the cut-off broom handle that Mum used to poke the rising washing back down into the boiling water in our copper, out the back of the washhouse. Otherwise, it would bubble over the side to be blackened on the charred outside of the copper. Then, of course, it would have to be taken back to the round galvanised iron tub in the washhouse and be washed all over again.

The time Dad knocked out the Rhode Island Red with the pot stick was the only time I recall it being used in violence. Frustration, perhaps, pent-up anger, or even to ward off a lonely mother's depression, but never, as I recall, in violence.

But that was only the start of the violence on that bright Saturday. At the woodheap there was one large block of hard-wood, probably iron bark, on which Dad would place the smaller bits of wood to split them and cut them to size for the stove when he was home on the occasional weekend.

It was also the block on which he laid the rooster's head before he chopped it off with one well-aimed blow of his razor-sharp Kelly axe. Then there was the hasty hold-out to arms-length by its horny legs as the blood spurted and sprayed from the severed neck and the poor bird, well its nerves anyway, twitched and jerked for what seemed ages after it should have been dead quiet.

That was the first time I'd seen a beheading.

It was a spectacle that I would not have understood at two, so I was probably curious, rather than horrified. I don't know how much a two-year-old understands about life and death. Do you? I can't remember how I felt.

In those days poultry was a luxury food item - usually on the menu only on festive occasions such as Christmas and Easter. And the Ingham brothers, Jack and Bob, who became multi-millionaires in the 1960's with their wholesale marketing of frozen chickens for Australian tables, were probably still boys in short pants.

Most working-class families kept chooks for their egg-laying, and at Easter and Christmas a couple of plump fowls would be chosen and there would be the ritual of decapitation, the hanging to bleed out and then the immersion of the carcass in boiling hot water in the copper to loosen the feathers for plucking. As I grew older, I began to accept the violence on the defenceless creatures because they were to end up on our dinner plates.

Were the chooks, turkeys or ducks - we kept them all most of the time - always killed on a Saturday? Probably not - especially with Christmas Day falling on just about any day of the week. But at Easter it was always Sunday that the Catholics celebrated and so the Sunday roast dinner was killed the day before, if Dad were home. He was the chook killer, and he was only ever home on the weekends - and that far from frequently. But he usually got home for Christmas at least, and sometimes for Easter as well. Anyway, we had only an ice chest for perishables back then, so it was usual to kill the chook the day before it was to be cooked.

When Dad was home, he would dress up on Saturday morning in a long-sleeved shirt - in summer rolled up to the elbows - a tie and his good hat. He was a tall, wiry man with a horseman's litheness, natural olive complexion deeply tanned from thirty years' exposure to the harsh Western Queensland outdoors. He'd left school at ten to go droving, and now he worked mainly as a stockman and horse-breaker on Stations around the district. It was how he met Mum. He went to Brisbane for treatment for a broken collarbone and met her in the kiosk at the Botanical Gardens. Downtown he would do the shopping that Mum asked him to do and then go to the pub, usually the Hotel Richards on the corner of Cambridge Street and Alice Street to "wet his whistle' as he called it. He would nearly always come home happy - a bit merry from the few beers and a catch-up with a mate or two. I never saw Dad stagger. Not like Angely Cochrane who broke his mother's heart by staggering home drunk one Good Friday.

Mum would make a salad - lettuce, tomato and crinkled cucumber - she used to scrape the peeled cucumber with the tines of a fork for some reason that I forget. The dressing was a kind of mayonnaise - condensed milk, mustard and vinegar were the main ingredients. With the salad we would have the cold meat Dad had brought home - sometimes sliced corned beef, but more often the cheaper Strasbourg or Windsor Sausage. We all sat at the table on the airy landing between the kitchen and the main house. Occasionally there would be jelly and custard or junket for "pudding" - but usually that was reserved for Sundays.

I always enjoyed Saturday lunch, and it was a bit special when Dad was home because we were all together for a change. Afterwards there was a whole afternoon of adventure for me.

One Saturday though I could hardly eat any lunch. Before Dad went down town we were supposed to be going to the Eastern Creek Rodeo in the afternoon.

All three of us children had showered and dressed in our Sunday best, and Mum had her best dress on too. When Dad came home, he walked in with his jaw set and an angry look on his face.

He dumped the few groceries on the kitchen table and announced that we were not going anywhere. When Mum protested that we kids had been looking forward to going and that it wasn't fair to change his mind, he became really angry. I don't know now what words passed between my parents, but I remember Dad holding his clenched right fist close to Mum's cheek and saying, 'A man ought to bloody well….'. I think that over the years I have deliberately forgotten the end of that sentence. I remember though the fear I felt at the back of my knees, and how hot and cramped the kitchen felt at that moment. Mum did not flinch or back away. She just said, 'You'll only do it once, Punch.' The irony of the word 'Punch' in that context was, of course, lost on me then. Punch was Dad's name. Everyone called him Punch. In his whole life I never heard anyone - even his sisters, Aunties Violet and Lily - call him, or refer to him, as "Henry" – which was his real name. On his memorial plaque beside Mum's in the Toowoomba Cemetery, it reads: Henry (Punch) Welch. I have always thought it was a mistake. It probably should read: Punch (Henry) Welch.

Anyway, next thing Dad was out at the wood heap in his good clothes, his tie flung over his shoulder, taking out his bad temper on the hard wood for the stove. Or was he doing a kind of penance for threatening Mum?

Mum made us sit up at the table and eat our lunch as if nothing had happened. That was Mum. 'Your father was not himself just then,' she said. And that was that. But I couldn't taste the food in front of me, and I hardly ate anything. I never saw or heard Dad threaten Mum again. Perhaps he remembered her calm warning about doing it only once. But I remember how that day our kitchen seemed suddenly too small.

Then, when I was a few years older, and could ride my black and green fixed wheel Malvern Star bike - even though it was too big for me - I was down town most Saturday afternoons. It may have been when I was earning some pocket money - two bob I think I got - for an afternoon of acting as "cockatoo" for Tommy Boland, the barber, who was an SP bookmaker. As his "cockatoo" I just had to hang around outside the barbershop and keep an eye out for the police. It was easy money - if a bit boring - especially when there were no sightings.

On those afternoons there would often be fights in or around the pubs. Men would have been drinking there from the ten o'clock opening time, and by mid-afternoon the grog would be starting to "talk" - loudly and sometimes aggressively. Next thing the drinkers would spill out through the batwing doors onto the street or, more often, round the back of the pub to watch the antagonists "settle things" with their bare fists.

While I loved listening to the boxing at the Brisbane Stadium on Friday nights on our little His Master's Voice battery mantel radio, I was repulsed by the raw violence of the bare-knuckle fist fights that took place behind the pubs in Mitchell most Saturday afternoons. The sound of bone crunching into bone and the sight of spurting blood was sickening.

I remember feeling nauseated as I watched a fight between Jacky Smart - a big overweight white shearer who lived at our end of town - and a much smaller, wiry, prematurely silver-haired half-caste, called Lewis Johnson. Johnson lived over the river at the Blacks' Camp which was called "The Yumba". Smart was a regular brawler - when drunk he enjoyed a fight more than a feed. Ironically, his wife was a tall, beautiful lady who was no doubt used to playing nurse most Saturday nights.

This day the big shearer was wearing a white, short-sleeved shirt, and brown, wide-legged, striped serge trousers and, of all things, sandals. He was a bit unsteady on his feet and his round-arm swings rarely landed. Johnson, on the other hand, calmly picked off his opponent with short, straight jabs and rips to his ample paunch, and upper cuts to his jaw. As he staggered back from a flurry of the smaller man's fists, one of Smart's sandals came off and he tripped. Next thing there was blood all over his white shirt, I just wanted it to stop and, thankfully, a few blows later it did. A couple of the more sober spectators stepped in to restrain Johnson who was standing threateningly over the prostrate Smart waiting for him to get up. So he could knock him down again.

Another Saturday afternoon when I was on watch outside Tommy Boland's barber shop, I saw the police coming along the footpath on the other side of the street. But I knew they wouldn't be troubling my bookmaker boss. There were two policemen - the Sergeant and the new young Constable - and they were frog-marching a big three-quarter caste dark man - Bob Hall, towards the watch-house. Although Hall was obviously pretty drunk, he was not going quietly, and the two police officers literally had their hands full. One moment the big man would pull back and try to sit on the pavement, the next he would charge forward almost pulling his captors off their feet. All the time he roared abuse at them.

As they made their erratic way around the corner of Ken Coorey's Manchester and Drapery store the big man managed to jerk his arms free. He lunged to his right in front of the off-balance Sergeant Bergen and pulled a paling off the Cooreys' garden fence. He managed to swing it effectively a couple of times and I could hear the whack and thud as it struck ribs and upper arms before "law and order" prevailed once more.

I could hardly wait to get home and tell Mum what I had seen. She was always on the side of the "darkies", and she had an Irish woman's suspicious view of the police. When I told her about the damage to Currie's fence and Bob Hall's brief but effective wielding of the paling she said, 'Good on him. They are always picking on the poor beggars. But they would have given him a terrible beating once they got him in the cell.'

Then there was the Saturday that Dad fought Arthur "Dicky" Mauritz near the big gate under the pine tree at the front of our yard.

Dad had been down town in the morning as usual - and he'd "wet his whistle" again. But he didn't come home relaxed and a bit merry. He strode inside and thrust the shopping on to the kitchen table as he had done the day we didn't go to the Eastern Creek Rodeo.

When Mum asked him what was wrong, he muttered something about '…. the bloody miserable old busy-body next door', tore off his tie and, rolling up his sleeves as he went, stormed back out the front door. He took no notice of Mum's pleas that he 'Come back and calm down. Don't be silly Punch. Nothing is worth fighting over. Come back and tell me what happened.'

He began shouting long before he got to the big gate at the corner of our boundary fence, 'Come out here you cherry-nosed old bastard!' It was true that Dicky Mauritz had a very round, very red nose. The rest though was just Dad's bad language and bad temper.

We kids didn't see the "fight" - Mum pushed us back inside and closed the front door. I don't think it lasted long - probably just a bit of push and shove - before Hec Carlyon, who was on his way to see Dad about breaking in a horse, stepped in and talked some sense into both of them.

But Dicky Mauritz must have got at least one good whack on Dad because he had a small split on the bridge of his nose. He lay down on the green, flowered linoleum in the hallway off the dining room - the only place where there was a slight breeze on that particularly hot afternoon. Mum gave him a couple of aspros for his headache and kept wetting a face-washer and waving it in the air to cool it before she laid it gently on his forehead. Waving the washer, she could have been a boxer's "second" trying to revive him for another round.

It turned out that Dad had met Brusher Clancy at the pub. Brusher owned the spooky house on the corner where I used to sleep with Dicky Mauritz's wife for a shilling a week when I was seven. Brusher had since pulled down a shed at the back of the house, and he had offered Dad the sheets of corrugated iron to cover a couple of day-yards for the horses at our stables in the back yard. Dicky had seen Dad bringing the iron home and assumed that he was probably stealing it. Why, I don't know. Dad wasn't a thief. Anyway, Dicky felt he had to let Brusher know that Dad had taken the iron. Of course, when Brusher told Dad, with a few drinks in him to stoke his outrage, Dad was hell-bent on teaching our busy-body neighbour a lesson.

The other violent Saturday I remember, and it horrified me, was when Fred Capel - a burly red-headed drover who was a newcomer to Mitchell - went berserk in the house diagonally across the road from our place. It was a little, cream-coloured house with a walled verandah. That is, instead of having a front verandah with railings and round palings like ours and many of the other houses in town, it had a chamferboard "wall" that came up rather higher than most railings.

Fred Capel was a daunting figure and, because he was often bad-tempered and shouting when he was in town and on the drink, I was always afraid of him.

I pitied his wife - a thin, nervy, red-headed woman who had some teeth missing, was usually shabbily-dressed, and often barefoot. Mum felt sorry for her too. She would often take over a pot of soup or some of the stew we were having that night and give it to her "for the children" - three or four little urchins who played outside in the dirt most of the day.

There was also a young man - probably eighteen or twenty - who lived with the Capels. I think he was a bit "simple", and I don't think I ever knew how he fitted into the family. Perhaps he was Mrs Capel's brother?

Anyway, late one Saturday afternoon, after a long "session", probably at several pubs, Capel began roaring and raging. Of course, I don't know what started it, other than the drink and the violence that appeared always imminent in Capel's presence. But what I remember quite vividly was seeing the big man grab the younger man and lift him in a horizontal position up to the height of his own red head before throwing him off the verandah into the front yard. It was an act of brute violence such as I had never seen, even at the "Flicks" - the Saturday afternoon matinees which we rarely attended.

The younger man landed flat on his back - in exactly the same position that Capel had hoisted him. He could have been dead and already stiff - but, to my great relief, he sat up after a few minutes and began to shake the sand out of his hair.

Early the following Monday there was cause for celebration. Fred Capel rounded up his horses before daylight and set off with his wagonette on another droving trip. I secretly hoped he would be going somewhere "over the border" and that he wouldn't be back for a long time. Ann Street felt much safer without him.

The next and final incident probably doesn't meet the entrance requirement for this story about violent Saturdays. It happened around five o'clock on a Thursday afternoon.

I was the last customer served at Tibby Blair's butcher shop that afternoon. I had once again been mulling over that official-looking notice on the back wall "No Smoking or Expectorating". The first part was clear enough to understand, but the last word I thought at the time must have something to do with women having babies. I could never quite pluck up the courage to ask Tibby to explain it.

Anyway, my attention and Tibby's was suddenly caught by shouting on the other side of the street - at the Downshire Arms Hotel. 'There must be a blue on,' said Tibby, coming round the end of the counter to my side. 'Let's see what's going on,' he added, pushing open the sprung front door and ushering me out onto the footpath with him.

We got outside just in time to see Ack Dawson, a local ringer and rouse-about who was another brawler in drink, come hurtling down the concrete steps to land on his back on the red gravel footpath in front of the pub. One side of his face was red raw - as if the skin had been peeled off it.

At the top of the stairs stood a nuggety, well-dressed man with a mat of thick, wavy red hair still perfectly combed and Brylcreem-ed.

'It's the Electrolux Man', said Tibby, 'I'll be buggered. He must be able to go a bit. Ack seems to have picked the wrong bloke this time.'

Back then, I mean when I was a boy in Mitchell, travelling salesmen would visit the town pretty regularly. They would arrive on the train, "The Western Mail" or the "Mail Train", as it was often called, and walk house-to-house selling their wares, often for a whole week. From time to time there would be Encyclopaedia Salesmen, Singer Sewing Machine Salesmen/Mechanics and, most popular with us kids, the Rawleighs man. He would sell all sorts of household items, but he specialised in medications – everything for the treatment of wounds or arthritic complaints, coughs, colds and fevers. Best of all he would have jellybeans, liquorice all-sorts or all-day suckers for the kids. They were the only items not labelled "Rawleighs".

And of course, there was the occasional visit by a vacuum cleaner salesman – especially after Mitchell became "electrified" after the war. Before that, only a few houses had power.

This vacuum cleaner salesman was newly arrived from England where he had probably done something else - as well as boxing. It turned out that since his recent arrival in Brisbane he had been earning his keep - at Snowy Hill's gym - as a sparring partner for the Aboriginal Australian Bantamweight Champion, Elley Bennett.

Tibby Blair was so right. Ack Dawson had apparently picked on the well-dressed little Englishman and called him a "sissy bloody Pom", among other things no doubt.

The vacuum cleaner salesman, no doubt weary after a day tramping the sandy footpaths of Mitchell, had ignored the bigger man's taunts for a long time. But when his tormentor walked along the bar and attempted to slap him over the ear, the "sissy Pom" cut loose with a bewildering array of well-aimed blows that soon saw the big man retreating, and ending up, as Tibby and I witnessed, on his back on the footpath.

Someone must have called the ambulance because Ack was carted off to hospital where he had a day or two to sober up and reflect on the danger of picking on "Sissy bloody Poms".

Looking back though, Mitchell was, like Banjo's Piper's Flat, a peaceful place during the week. And not every Saturday was marked by violence. I think the fact that Saturday was most commonly the day of violence could be attributed to the fact that many of the men worked out of town - in shearing sheds and on cattle stations. They would get to town on Friday night and many of them would quench a week's hard-earned thirst on Saturday at one or more of the five pubs. By afternoon many of them would not be thinking straight. Some could not "hold their grog" and would be looking to fight, or to start one between two or more others.

But Mitchell was something of a frontier town in those days - rather like the Australia that Henry Lawson depicted in his portraits of bush life. My mother and "The Drover's Wife" had a lot in common. And, just as in Lawson's works, there was kindness and generosity that far outweighed the occasional cruelty and violence that erupted most frequently on Saturdays in my old home town.

.

WHEN THE WAR WAS ON

Life in Mitchell, like everywhere else no doubt, was different. Well, it was different from the life after the war. And I'm sure it was different from the life before the war although I can't remember much about that period. I was only two when the war broke out.

I had nothing to do with it either. I wasn't sure about how it all started, but I thought the Germans probably did it. Most of the grown-ups I knew said that Germany's leader, Adolph Hitler, was a madman who wanted to conquer the world. He had a big group of followers called Nazis. I thought at first that the word was German for "Nasties."

Anyway, this is not military history really. It is just about life in Mitchell when the war was on. It is hard to know where to start. So, I will just plunge in – probably in the wrong place – but one has to start somewhere.

The shortages. There were many things that you couldn't buy in the shops. Probably because the countries we imported them from were too busy defending themselves to go on producing them. All over the world countries were engaged in what was called on the radio and in the Saturday Newsreels at the pictures, "the war effort."

Even the things produced here in Australia were in short supply. So, every family had a ration book. The ration book was a small item of soft cardboard or durable thick paper divided by dotted, easy-tear lines into probably twenty detachable coupons per page. It was issued at the Post Office on a monthly basis, I think.

What I am sure of is that it was one of Mum's most precious possessions. When I was little, and Walter would take me to the shops Mum would always give the ration book to Walter to look after.

Groceries such as butter, sugar, flour, rice and tea were rationed. That meant that you not only had to pay for them, but you had to hand over the requisite number of coupons as well. A pound of butter probably cost one and six (a shilling and sixpence), but it cost coupons as well. People had to be careful with their purchases, because once all the coupons were used up you couldn't buy any of those rationed goods.

When we ran out of coupons and there was no butter in the house, Mum would buy some suet from the butcher's and render it down to a greyish spread. It certainly wasn't as tasty as real butter, but it was better than eating dry toast at breakfast. People learned to "make do" when the war was on.

To make Mitchell less vulnerable to bombing attacks at night people pasted newspaper over their windows. It made the inside of the house a bit drab by day, but people probably slept better at night because they felt safer.

That reminds me of another shortage – kerosene. I think it was in short supply because of the need for aviation fuel. The Air Force was heavily engaged in battles on the other side of the world and in New Guinea, as well as defending Australia from airstrikes – especially after the bombing of Darwin.

In Mitchell most houses relied on kerosene for lighting, and a few, who could afford it, refrigeration. We only had an ice-chest, so we didn't need "kero" for a fridge. And we overcame the shortage for lighting by getting a carbide light.

The carbide light was a strange, sturdy contraption consisting of a galvanised cylinder and a couple of burners. The burners were like two little horns facing inwards atop a straight, hollow stem. You put the carbide (it looked like little grey rocks and had an acrid smell that got up your nose and made your eyes water) in the bottom of the cylinder and filled it to a certain level with water. The carbide, which had a pungent, almost flammable smell when it was dry, reacted strongly with the water – hissing, gurgling, and forming a gas. The gas rose through the central hollow stem and emerged from the pin holes in the twin burners. It burned with a surprisingly bright glow that gave a light comparable with our good kerosene table lamp, and better than our hurricane lantern.

The only problem with a carbide light was its tendency to explode. Luckily, it always began to splutter and spurt before it went right off. It must have been towards the end of the war that we had to use carbide lights because it was my job when it started to splutter, to grab the thing and hurl it onto the lawn where it could erupt safely. I could not have done that when I was only two or three. Mum wouldn't have let me do it back then, but by the time we had the carbide lights I was old enough for her to say, 'Quick Merv, throw it as far as you can.'

On the lawn it would splutter a bit more, convulse a few times and then, probably because we were all safely out of range, give up and lie quite tamely on its side.

Another thing about Mitchell when the war was on was that we had air-raid shelters. There was one in every back-yard and a really big one in the playground at St Patrick's Convent School.

Neighbours helped one another to dig the ones behind the houses. Bung Carlyon, who was Dad's partner in the tank-sinking business helped Dad and Dad helped Bung, and a few of our other close neighbours.

A veritable army of fathers dug the big one at school. Luckily, Mitchell was on a sandy plain, so the pick and shovel digging was usually relatively easy. Still, those trenches were quite deep, and I can remember the sweat pouring off the men's faces and dripping off their noses. For some weird reason I wished I could sweat like that – but it's hard to sweat when you are little. And when I was old enough to work up a sweat it soon lost its fascination.

We didn't have air-raid practice at home, but we did most days at school. One of the nuns would ring the school bell and for once, it was a pleasure to hear it. It meant that we would be out of class for the length of the air-raid drill – usually at least half an hour. It would be 'Stand up! Seats back!' We sat on stools that seated about five of us at long wooden desks that had a hinged, sloping surface which we lifted up to store our work pads, atlases and School Readers, holes for ink wells and long shallow grooves to hold our pencils and pens.

Once on our feet we would have to 'Move briskly in an orderly manner,' to the back stairs. Then we would practise marching, without panic, down the stairs and over to the air-raid shelter. A couple of the big boys would have removed part of the roof over the trench so we could descend into the cool safety below. When the last of us was safely stowed, the roof boys would come down and manoeuvre the removeable section of the roof back into place. Then it was darkness and silence.

Although it was only a practice session, there was always an air of excitement about it – as if we were really a part of the war. We weren't allowed to talk, even in a whisper. I'm not quite sure why. Surely, we couldn't be heard by the imagined Japanese kamikaze fighter pilots, even if they came in low over the Convent roof.

Anyway, it always seemed too soon when the bell rang, and we had to leave our, by now, very stuffy haven below the playground.

One of the shortages I forgot to mention was dates. They were not really a shortage because you couldn't buy them at all. It was probably because they were imported from Egypt and a few other countries where date palms grew in desert-like conditions.

Dates came back into the shops sometime after the war, but they were rationed for quite a long while. I'm not sure if you still had to use coupons to buy dates, but I remember that there were limits – like a maximum of a pound of dates per family per month.

Imagine Mum's reaction when I got home from the shops with what was our first pound of post-war dates. Well, not with the whole pound. The dates arrived at the grocery store, Short and Hobson's, in large bags about the size of a sugar bag. Jacky Hunter or Billy Lees, whoever was serving you that day, would use a scoop to ladle out the allowed weight into a brown paper bag. Back then, brown paper, dispensed from large rolling guillotines was the main wrapping material, and brown paper bags were used for all sorts of loose items like rice, sugar, potatoes and, now that they had become available, dates.

The problem with brown paper bags was that the top was just rolled down; so, a curious or hungry boy could easily access the contents.

So it was that our first pound of dates was considerably reduced by the time I'd carried the groceries the mile and a half from Short and Hobson's in Cambridge Street to our little brown house near the end of Ann Street. Mum, who loved me dearly, suffered a temporary lapse of maternal devotion.

In Mitchell, as in most other towns in Australia I suppose, there was a group of men in what was called the VDC – the Voluntary Defence Corps. They were to be the last line of defence, if and when the Japanese Army came to capture Mitchell. The VDC did military exercises every second Sunday at the rifle range over the river on the northern side of the railway line. They practised marching drills, dropping on their bellies, rifles at the ready and firing blanks. I suppose they were the prototype for "Dad's Army," the popular television comedy series which immortalised in satire their bumbling defence capabilities.

I remember the big boys at school treating our local VDC as something of a joke. They used to say things like: 'They only go over the river to "play soldiers," much as we did to play "Cowboys and Indians", and 'If the Japs really did get here, the VDC would probably head for the hills and order the rest of us to follow.' It was hard to know which way we would be going though, because Mitchell sits on a vast sandy plain. I supposed we would head out past the hospital because it was just off the road to St George that there was a hill where Dad said the police captured the Kenniffs. The Kenniffs were bushrangers in the area before I was born.

Anyway, I'm sure the VDC were good men with the best of intentions. Luckily, the Japs never did get as far south as Mitchell, or even Cape York, so we never found out if the big boys were right.

Another thing that happened when the war was on was the arrival of American soldiers. There was a military air base in Charleville and a fairly large group of American soldiers stationed in Mitchell. Was it a single platoon? I'm not sure now. But a few things stand out in my memory. One was that we kids were a bit scared of the big negro soldiers. Looking back now I'm sure it was just their imposing physiques and almost purple blackness that caused our fear. Generally, the soldiers were friendly and generous, and I think we all felt a bit safer because of their presence. But it also brought the war closer to our town.

We were amazed at the equipment they had – the jeeps (some of them amphibious and hardly necessary in Mitchell), huge troop transports and assorted military machinery. I don't remember if there were any tanks. One Sunday there was some kind of military gymkhana at the "rec" – the local recreation grounds which was home to

Mitchell Rugby League, Cricket and Tennis.

It was an exciting day as the "Yanks," as the American soldiers were irreverently and fondly called, put their military machinery through their paces.

One of the demonstrations was to show how quickly they could set up lines of communication by installing telephone lines. The machine that dug the holes for the poles was a massive auger. It dug a hole ten or twelve feet deep in three or four seconds. Some of the town youths had fun dropping into the holes and being hoisted to the surface by a mobile crane.

Anthony Doonan, a sixteen-year-old, red-haired, freckled young fellow who boarded with us at the time, took his turn in the hole. That night, about ten o'clock, Mum heard groans coming from the back bedroom where Anthony slept. She hurried in with the lantern to find him having a fit or taking a seizure. I remember seeing him frothing at the mouth and shaking, with only the whites of his eyes showing. It was the first time I had seen anything like that. It was certainly different from what happened to me in the old church when we were rehearsing the play "Who Killed Cock Robin?" Perhaps Mrs Marshall was right. I probably had just fainted.

Anyway, Anthony was extremely ill. He had contracted meningitis, and, after months in hospital "down below," he recovered but was left totally deaf. So, he had to give up his electrician's apprenticeship and he could not ride a bike anymore. That's how I came to get his black and green, fixed-wheel, full-sized Malvern Star bicycle. Mum and Dad bought it from Anthony's parents who had moved to Brisbane some months previously. That is why Anthony was boarding with us.

Mum thought at the time of his taking ill that Anthony may have picked up a germ from the soil when he was down the hole.

I know that the Anthony Doonan story was not really a war story, but it happened when the war was on and it happened on the day, well the night really, of the American Military Gymkhana. So Anthony Doonan may have been one wartime casualty that was unreported and completely overlooked. But there was one local casualty associated with the American military deployment in Mitchell that saddened the whole town. It was the accidental death of a little boy, David Lansdowne, who was run over by a jeep. It was a tragic accident and I remember Mum and other people expressing sympathy for the young driver who was apparently in grief-stricken shock. I think David Lansdowne was his parents' only son. He may have been their only child. I'm not sure now.

But what I do remember clearly is his funeral. With all the American military vehicles, and almost every family car in Mitchell district in line, it seemed the procession would never end. Mum wouldn't let us count the cars at a funeral and most times it was a disappointment because for us kids, watching from our backyard, it was usually the most interesting thing.

Though I didn't count the cars at little David Lansdowne's funeral, I think it may have set a record that still stands. But I suspect that Mum's rule about not counting the cars was a widely observed taboo and no such records were kept. So no-one would know for sure, and if they did, they would probably be too old to remember.

Thinking of the sad times when the war was on reminds me that Saturdays were anxious days for Mitchell people with family members fighting overseas. Saturday was the day they would go to the Post Office to scan the lists of those missing in action, or worse, killed in battle in places like Borneo and New Guinea.

I remember the Saturday when Jim McCreath was listed as being killed in battle. Mrs McCreath was quite a bit older than Mum and I think Jim was her only son. I don't remember a Mr McCreath so Mrs McCreath may have been a widow. Anyway, Mum was a good friend of

Jim's sisters, Elsie and Belle, and she knew the family would be heartbroken by the terrible news. Mum's eyes were red for days after that awful Saturday.

One other thing that happened on Saturdays was the picture show, or "the flicks" as they were called. At the Maranoa Theatre, with its row upon row of canvas chairs – like dozens of squatter's chairs joined together, there was a matinee on Saturday afternoon and another show at night.

One of the features that preceded the main program, usually two full-length feature films separated by a ten- or fifteen-minute interval, was the Movietone News.

It was a newsreel that gave progress reports on the war - especially in the Pacific and regions close to Australia. I suppose it was a bit out of date by the time it got to the Maranoa Theatre, but it was always dramatic to see what the war was actually like.

Another thing I remember about the war years was the rivalry between Australian service men and the American troops – marines they were often called.

The American soldiers, sailors and airmen all wore uniforms that appeared more stylish than the Aussie Digger clobber. Their cocky-looking berets were apparently more appealing than the slouch hat pinned up on one side with the rising sun badge.

Apart from that, the American troops seemed to have an endless supply of cigarettes (Lucky Strikes and Camels), chewing gum, and – probably most alluring to the single Aussie "sheilas" – nylon stockings.

For us kids the chewing gum was a novel experience and taste. We were used to the small packets of Wrigley's PKs and Juicy Fruit – the chewing gum packaged in little white pillows of sugary enamel. The American variety came in strips about three inches long and half an inch wide. It was fawn in colour and lightly coated with a sweetish powder. It did not have that initial burst of sweetness as your teeth broke through the enamel of the PK and began to crunch it up. But there was a pleasing "chewiness" in the texture of the American gum and the flavour, though not quite as sweet, lasted longer than that of the Wrigley's versions.

As for the Lucky Strikes and the nylon stockings, I cannot speak or recall with any authority. I was just turning eight when the war ended. I think the cigarettes were considerably stronger than the Capstan and Ardath Specials that Australians were used to smoking. And nylon stockings were either a novelty or a very scarce commodity in the war years. They were, in any case, a strong attraction for Australian girls and probably a significant causal element in the "Battle of Brisbane" - a violent brawl that occurred one night between the Allies – the Australian and American troops. Was that a kind of civil war? It went on for several days.

When the war ended there was a big celebration out on the plain near the bore that supplied Mitchell's water. The town was very proud of its bore water – bubbling up from the artesian, or is it the sub-artesian basin? In summer the water can get too hot to stand under in the shower. But it is a boon in the winter when Mitchell can rival Stanthorpe at times for the title of the coldest town in Queensland.

Anyway, when people who had moved away from Mitchell returned later to live there, it was said that it was the bore water that brought them back. I don't think the same could have been said for Roma's water. The first time I smelled Roma water in a wash basin at the Commonwealth Hotel it reminded me of rotten eggs. But water had little to do with the peace party out on the plain under the starry western sky. I'm not sure why the party was held out there, but perhaps it was because there was a huge bonfire and fireworks. There was no chance that a fire could get away out there on that grassless plain.

Just about the whole town was out there singing and dancing. My teenage cousin, George (Porge) Rashford was there, looking after me - when he wasn't flirting with some pretty girl. The Rashfords had been our next-door neighbours before they moved "down below" - to Gatton. George must have been back in Mitchell and staying with us for a holiday. He was the likeable larrikin of the large Rashford family. The Rashfords never moved back to Mitchell as a family, but one of the brothers, John, came back and stayed. I never asked him if it was the bore water that drew him back.

I remember that peace celebration clearly. For once, everyone seemed to be equal. The police sergeant, the bank manager, the shop owners, the schoolteachers all joined in the singing, hugging and laughing with the rest.

They did a dance called the Conga – which was like a long, disabled snake. They formed a line, one behind the other, each person holding on to the hips of the person in front. Then, to the tune of some popular war-time song like "It's a long way to Tipperary," or "You take the high road and I'll take the low road" – they did a hoppy kind of dance, kicking the free leg out to the side with every step. The kids joined on the end.

Sometime after the war ended there was a "welcome home" tribute to the brave Mitchell men who had served in the war. A kind of ticker-tape reception I suppose it was. The returned soldiers, sailors and airmen were driven in open flat-backed trucks through town to the "rec" – the Mitchell Sports and Recreation Ground.

I remember a few of the Mitchell men who served in the war and were honoured that day. But I won't mention their names because I can't remember all of the others. They were all our local heroes, and it would hardly be fair to single out the few I can recall.

Mum shed a few tears that day. She was no doubt thinking of those who didn't return – especially Jim McCreath.

Shortly after the war, the "Balts" arrived in Mitchell. They were groups of big, blonde, raw-boned refugees from Czechoslovakia, Yugoslavia, Finland and Denmark - countries that had been ravaged by the war.

In Mitchell they worked in gangs on Council projects. They were silent, strong men who kept pretty much to themselves - probably because they couldn't speak English. It would not have helped that Mitchell people were unused to having "New Australians" living and working in the town. Not that Mitchell people were inhospitable, but probably they didn't really know how to overcome the language barriers, and the "Balts" seemed to be contented in their own small community.

Their counterparts, fellow refugees from all over Europe, working on the Snowy River Scheme became famous and honoured in Australian history. But the Balts who worked in the Mitchell heat were unremarked and probably largely forgotten. I'm not even sure now what they did. Perhaps they worked on the bituminising of the main street, putting the power on, or was it the Mitchell sewerage scheme?

I don't think any of them stayed on in Mitchell when their tour of duty ended.

They were, in a way, the last living reminders of the war years.

THE FIRST CUT IS THE DEEPEST

We had been sweethearts for three or four years. She was blonde and very pretty, with large wide-set blue eyes and high cheekbones. Her hair was thick and wavy, and she had a shapely, well-developed figure.

Her slim waist she accentuated with the wide shirred waistbands on the full-flared skirts that were the fashion in the early fifties.

Daphne was talented too - made most of her own clothes and did a lot of the cooking for her family - her parents, a sister Shirley and brother Neville, both younger than she was.

Her father, Bill Taylor, was a strict and domineering head of the family. At thirteen I was afraid of him and pleased that he was a bit of a recluse. He never came to the Saturday night dances with his wife and children, and I don't recall seeing him much around the town.

Saturday nights were the highlights of the week for me and for most of the young people in Mungallala. There was usually a dance held in the corrugated iron hall with the well-worn dance floor. Often the dance would be in aid of one of the local organisations - the Progress Association, the Younger Set - ironically run and kept together by the town's much-loved seventy-something matriarch, Granny Sallway - the Cricket Club or the Christmas Tree Committee.

Mungallala's Christmas Tree Dance in early December was famous throughout the surrounding districts, and families came - literally - by the truckload to enjoy it. Every child got a present from Santa, there was always a lavish supper, and the dancing went on into the wee hours. Infants and pre-schoolers would be sleeping in baskets and on make-shift "swags" under the seats around the walls of the hall.

Many of the men would not turn up until after Clancy's pub shut at ten o'clock. Apparently the "session" gave them what they called "Dutch Courage" - making them game enough to ask the women for a dance. It was amazing how well most of them danced - considering they were probably "three sheets in the wind".

Anyway, the Saturday dance was my chance to be with Daphne, to hold her close in the waltzes and squeeze her hand as we waited for the next bracket to begin. It was then that I felt I was the luckiest boy in the world.

Of course, I had to have a dance or two with my younger sisters, Maureen and Lola, and a dance with Mum. She would usually suggest I ask some girl who wasn't getting many dances. The rest of the night and always for the Medley - the last dance of the night - I would dance with Daphne. I was past the stage of caring about being teased for having a girlfriend. I was in love and could not think of anything better than marrying Daphne and having lots of kids.

In February 1951 I went to boarding school in Toowoomba and Daphne went off to Moreton Bay College for Girls in Brisbane. The separation only inflamed my ardour. It's the old saying "Absence makes the heart grow fonder".

It was difficult to maintain contact as at my school our letters, written on Sunday mornings in the study hall between eleven am and 12 noon, had to be handed in to Father Bell, the supervising priest, in addressed but open envelopes. All our letters were "vetted" before posting.

So, there was no chance of writing a genuine love-letter. I remember Father Bell calling me to his room to discuss the mysterious "Daphne" whom I had addressed as "cousin" in the letter under scrutiny, a couple of times. I don't think he was totally convinced by my "explanation". For one thing he wanted to know why she was attending a non-Catholic boarding school. That was a particularly sticky problem, because in the 1950s the "Great Divide" between Catholics and Protestants was very evident. To make matters worse at Downlands - the other boys in my class knew I had a girlfriend and that her name was Daphne. "Irene Goodnight" was a hit song in the early 50s and on bus trips there would always be a complete rendition, to my embarrassment, of "Daphne Goodnight".

Mum was Catholic and the kids were raised Catholic and educated at Catholic schools, but Dad was a non-practising Protestant.

I'm not sure if he was ever christened in any particular faith. I always knew though that, as a family, we were not quite as valued by the nuns and the Parish Priest as were the families that were united in the "one true faith" and turned up as a family to Sunday Mass.

Daphne was not a Catholic - but that was not a consideration for me. I loved her. And I would have either got her to convert to Catholicism or married her "behind the altar" - as was the fate of those couples who dared to enter the "dangerous waters" of a mixed-marriage. But we would marry, and in my innocent, romantic imagination, we would live happily ever after.

For those first two years of secondary schooling we kept our romance intact by the occasional letter and of course by as much contact as we could manage in the school holidays. That wasn't all that satisfactory though - as old Bill, her father, kept a tight rein on his growing daughters.

I was never invited home to Daphne's place - her father would not have tolerated it. Her mother was different - a kindly, shy, red-haired lady who I suspected was pretty much under her husband's thumb.

One occasion I remember though, particularly vividly. Daphne was allowed to come to our place one Sunday and I took her riding. I had a smart grey Galloway, of which I was quite proud, and Daphne was riding one of our reliable stockhorses - a black horse we called Jake. We dismounted after riding an hour or so away from home and sat down in the shade on the edge of a dry Sandy Creek. I put my arm around Daphne and accidentally cupped her right breast with my hand.

Being a good Catholic lad, I immediately apologised, and years later I realised it was probably a terrible mistake - the apology I mean.

After Junior - Year 10 nowadays - Daphne left school and went to work in Sallway's General Store, one of only two shops in Mungallala. The other was Greg Young's Café. I went back to Downlands College to complete my senior studies and to prepare for a career in teaching.

I went home for the Christmas holidays at the end of my second last year of boarding school, and Daphne's first year in the "adult" world of work, and, in comparison to school life, "freedom".

It was Saturday, and the Christmas Tree Dance was on that night. I could hardly wait to get there - I'd been to the store that morning of course - but the shop was busy, and Daphne didn't have much time to talk.

That night she looked outrageously beautiful, in a waist-hugging floral flared skirt, and pretty, white, lace-trimmed cotton blouse.

But there was something different about her. It was not just that she seemed more grown-up - "adult" I should say. It was there when we danced. Her body seemed less relaxed - somehow more distant than it had ever felt before. You can sense that when you dance with someone - they are relaxed and "with you", or they are holding you - literally - at arm's length. Anyway, I remember being aware of a change that I did not understand or like.

I asked if I could have the Medley, the last dance which was usually taken as permission to take the girl home. She agreed, and I was somewhat reassured as I had never walked her home before. We walked hand-in-hand making small talk until we reached the big, old gum tree some sixty or seventy yards from her front gate.

The light was on in the house, so her mother and probably old Bill were waiting for her to come in. I was nervous, but I didn't want to let her go - I think I feared the worst.

I asked her straight-out if there was somebody else. She looked away as she said there was - a man called Colin Taylor. I knew him as a local "ringer". He would have been in his early to mid-twenties then - a tall, dark and handsome shearer.

I guess I knew at once that I could not compete - even though I was a much better dancer. To confirm that she had outgrown me, or perhaps to show what real lovers do, when she kissed me goodnight, she put her strong and lively tongue in my mouth. It was a shock!

It was the first time I had ever been kissed like that. Ironically it had not the usual effect of excitement and anticipation that I have since at times enjoyed - but rather a sense of cold finality, of my being discarded because I wasn't worldly enough, because I didn't know the ways of women.

My heart broke for the first time sixty-six years ago.

ABOUT THE AUTHOR

Merv Welch lives with his wife in a regional town in Queensland. A teacher by profession, he has instilled in several generations of students a love of verse and stories – stories told 'straight out of his mouth' as one young lad remarked - meaning stories told from memory, not read from the pages of a book. His writing is very much in his own voice, both humorous and personable. Now in his eighties, Merv retains his sense of humour, his love of family and his connection with many life-long friends. This is the first of a series of volumes yet to be published.